He Saw
a
Hummingbird

*Norma Lee Browning
and
Russell Ogg*

PRESS

Northwood Institute Press

Midland, Michigan

For information contact: Northwood Institute Press
Midland, Michigan 48640

Library of Congress Cataloging in Publication Data

Browning, Norma Lee.
   He saw a hummingbird.

   1. Browning, Norma Lee. 2. Photographers—United States—Biography. 3. Diabetic retinopathy—Biography.
I. Ogg, Russell, joint author. II. Title.
TR140.B785B76   770'.92'4 [B]   78-2559

ISBN: 0-87359-043-0

10   9   8   7   6   5   4   3   2

Reprint of
FIRST EDITION

To Caroline Rogers Richardson . . .
For her vision and vigilance which sustained
us and brought this book to fruition . . .

．．．

And to Ruth Miller . . .
A very special Hummingbird friend . . .
With love

Contents

Acknowledgments

As a veteran newspaper reporter covering many tough assignments over the years, I must confess this one was the most difficult, not only because of its very personal nature but because my husband was an unwilling subject. When I first took his hummingbird pictures to New York to show to editors and publishers, and then called to tell him we were going to do a book, his initial reaction was, "You didn't tell them about my eyes, did you?"

If they wanted the hummingbird pictures, fine; but he strongly opposed the idea of baring our personal lives to the public. At one point he told me to forget the whole thing. Only through the constant encouragement and persuasion of many friends and professional people alike was he finally convinced, albeit reluctantly, that his story should be told as an inspiration to others.

We wish to express our grateful appreciation to Marian Skedgell whose skillful and sensitive editorial guidance was largely responsible for this book ever seeing the light of day.

For help in our hummingbird research we would like to thank Mary Fahr of the Palm Springs Public Library who went to great trouble to find hard-to-find books and scientific papers for us; Dr. Robert and Mrs. (Marjorie Pohl) White, longtime "birders" who introduced us to the intricacies of hummingbird species identification; Donald and Ella Woods who scouted humming-bird books, nests, and flowers for us.

We are indebted to many whose published works provided invaluable guideposts to our own hummingbird watching. Notably among them: Crawford H. Greenewalt, Augusto Ruschi, Walter Scheithauer, Alexander F. Skutch, Roger Tory Peterson.

And to a dear man, Mike Kennedy, a former editor of The Chicago Tribune, who stood by us through the early rough times.

We owe a very special debt of gratitude to certain friends who were always there when we needed them, or would come on a moment's notice to lend a hand and a pair of good eyes in the darkroom: Photographers Ray Jones, Gary Julius, Lee Thomas; also Fran and Al Ligier, Hazel and Al Kidder, Pam Gallagher and Gordon Hansen, Lynda and Dick White, and our former Girl Friday assistant on many assignments, Vera Servi, who has lived this one with us from its beginning.

Acknowledgments

Finally, with affection and esteem, we thank Mr. and Mrs. W. Clement Stone who have been a constant source of encouragement and inspiration; Mrs. Joseph E. Maddy and all our friends at the Interlochen Fine Arts Academy; the doctors and nurses who played a most important role in this story.

Just as hummingbirds are "glittering fragments of the rainbow," as Audubon called them, so it takes many threads to weave a tapestry, whether in fine arts or life.

Our thanks to all who helped make this book possible.

Palm Springs   Norma Lee Browning
September 1978   Russell Ogg

POSTSCRIPT, May 1984

By popular request our book is being re-issued by the Northwood Institute Press. We wish to express our grateful appreciation to Northwood's co-founders, Dr. Arthur E. Turner and Dr. R. Gary Stauffer; Dr. David E. Fry, president and John A. Church, senior vice president, Virginia Morrison and Don Th. Jaeger.

Also to Tom and Debbie Collazo, managers of the Mile Hi Nature Conservancy in Ramsey Canyon, Arizona, where we are currently working on a videofilm of the hummingbirds. . . . And a very special thank-you to Marjorie Taylor and all of you who have read our book and passed along its message to others; also to God for creating hummingbirds and giving a blind man the gift of vision to photograph them.

N.L.B.
R.J.O.

CHAPTER ONE

The Dream

Last night I dreamed he caught a hummingbird.

It was that same haunting dream again, always in iridescent colors, like glittering fragments of a rainbow.

Always the same little gossamer-winged, red-headed hummer, the one we named Little Redbird, the one who flew away and never came back.

But in the recurring dream he comes back, hovering and whirring in the man's gentle hands as though to say, "Here I am. Can you see me now?"

The man's eyes follow the red flash of color as it darts in the bright sunlight among the oleanders and orange blossoms, then streaks off toward the mountains.

I awaken and I know that it was only a dream. But it was

1

spun from reality. It is part of a once-upon-a-time story that really happened, with perhaps the promise of a happily-ever-after ending.

For once upon a time there really was a little red hummer.

And there really is a man who still listens for the whir of hummingbird wings, whose eyes strain and search among the rainbow colors, and who sometimes says wistfully, "I'd know him if I ever saw him again."

The man is my husband.

Before he saw the hummingbird, my husband, a photographer, was going blind. His medical records show that today he is, in fact, legally blind.

Russell's loss of sight was caused by diabetic retinopathy. He has been a severe diabetic, living on daily injections of insulin, for more than thirty-six years—since January 1942.

At the University of Missouri we had been campus sweethearts, but I had gone on to Radcliffe for my master's and was starting on my Ph.D. when Russell, with fifteen dollars in his pocket and a camera slung over one shoulder, hitchhiked fifteen hundred miles from Missouri. He announced that I had stayed in school long enough. So we were married—in a small chapel in Harvard Square.

Three years later, while were were on our first assignment as a writer-photographer team in the grapefruit orchards of Mc-

Allen, Texas, Russell collapsed without warning and was rushed to a hospital in a diabetic coma.

We did not even know what diabetes was until the doctor told us, after Russell came out of his coma.

"You're lucky to be alive," he said, rather perfunctorily, and gave us a pamphlet to read. "You'll have to live on insulin—three shots a day. You have to watch out for complications. Blindness and amputations, they're the two biggest problems. There's a woman in here now, a diabetic, we just amputated her leg. You have to take care of your feet. . . ."

He brought out a hypodermic needle and a bottle of insulin and started to explain to me how to give the insulin shots to my husband.

I fainted.

But it was the first and only time.

Russell was in and out of hospitals for five years, with various complications, before we realized that his diabetes was different. Puzzled doctors would shake their heads, try a different type of insulin or a different dosage, change his diet, and recommend another diabetic specialist. We were willing to try anything. On our doctor's recommendation Russell agreed to spend a month in the diabetic clinic of one of the country's leading medical university hospitals, submitting to various tests and experiments. These were done under inflexibly controlled conditions and included a strict regimen of supervised activity, weighed foods, varied insulin-diet-drug combinations. We were surprised when he was dismissed at the end of two weeks—instead of a month —with instructions to come to the clinic director's office after he checked out.

The first doctor in McAllen had warned us, "You're not a mild case." The diabetic specialist now put it in more specific terms and in words that made a deep impact on my husband.

"Unfortunately, you happen to be one of those brittle diabetics we can't do anything about. You'll have to learn to control it yourself."

We hadn't expected a miracle. We knew there was no cure for diabetes; insulin is not a cure, as many people believe. Insulin only allows a diabetic to live from day to day. But the amount of insulin must be regulated with diet and physical activity in order to control the diabetic's blood sugar.

There are approximately 10 million diabetics in the United States. My husband's case is not at all typical. In the vast majority of cases the disease *can* be controlled by insulin and diet.

Russell was discouraged at first, but soon he accepted his condition as something he had to live with—and not worry about. He had to take care of himself, and he did a pretty good job of it. There were still blackouts and emergency trips to the hospital, baffled doctors and interminable tests for this and that, but he refused to let it get him down.

He had a fetish about not discussing his "health problem," as he called it. "No one wants to hear about other people's problems. They have their own problems," is the way he put it. After one excursion to a hospital he remarked, "It's a little inconvenient, but you get accustomed to it."

One day Russell's doctor telephoned me and asked me to come to his office. Russell was in the hospital again, this time in Chicago, and I knew the doctor's call meant the problem was serious.

"Unfortunately," he began. . . . I had heard that word many times before, but this time it had a more ominous ring. He tried to prepare me. "I'm afraid I have bad news. . . . The life expectancy of the average diabetic is reduced 30 percent. Your husband has been lucky so far. . . ."

"How long do you expect him to live?"

"*If* we pull him through this one," he said cautiously. "We can't make predictions."

"What do you mean, *if* you pull him through?" I asked.

"His blood sugar count is 450. You realize what that means."

I understood. My husband might soon die in a diabetic coma.

"If he comes out of it this time, how long will he live?" No one had ever told me, and I felt I was entitled to know.

"I'd say two, three, five years at the most."

About a week after he came home from the hospital, Russell announced at the breakfast table, "I'm going to the South Pacific. Would you like to go with me?"

I thought he was joking. When I found out he wasn't, I told

him about my conversation with the doctor and begged him not to go.

"Look," he said, "you can't sit around feeling sorry for yourself just because you have a health problem. I'm not going to stop doing things I want to do just because a doctor says I'm going to die someday. If I worried about that, I'd be worried every time I crossed the street; I could be hit by a bus and die tomorrow. I happen to have a disease and I have to live with it, but I don't intend to let it run my life. And I don't intend to die very soon," he added.

Within a month we had sublet our apartment, sold our house in northern Michigan, quit our jobs, and were on our way to Tahiti in a rust-bucket freighter. We roamed around the South Sea Islands by freighter and copra boats for a year and a half, then came back to better jobs, built a new house, and found another doctor. The one who had warned us about Russell's life expectancy had died of a heart attack.

That was twenty-five years ago.

Since then Russell has brightened more hospital corridors than I care to remember, confounding medical staffs with his resilience and his refusal to stay dead or dying when they thought he was or should be.

On one occasion the nurses who checked his morning laboratory reports found his blood sugar count down to 28. (About 160 is considered normal.) Alarmed, they called the doctor, then rushed to Russell's room to find him doing his morning exercises.

The Dream

"He gave us a bit of a scare this time," one nurse said, "but we love having him for a patient. We wish they were all like him."

Russell has a special knack for making everyone feel, while he's in a hospital, that *this* particular hospital is the best place in the world to be.

But that's the rosy side of the picture. There are darker realities in the life of a diabetic.

Popular myth to the contrary, to live as a diabetic isn't merely a matter of not eating cake and pie and ice cream and of taking your insulin shots every day. A minor cold can quickly shoot the blood sugar up, and bring on pneumonia or a coma. The tiniest bruises or scratches take a long time healing and can lead to infections or other complications. A splinter in the hand, a stubbed toe, a cut on the leg can cause serious problems.

Too much or too little insulin, too much or not enough food, too much time between insulin and food, too much or too little exercise or physical activity—all of these can cause the blood sugar to rise or fall. I doubt if there is a diabetic alive who hasn't experienced the dry-lips, thick-tongue, trembling, sweating symptoms of insulin reaction. I've often had to call in our next-door neighbor to help me pick up my husband from the floor and get the sugar water down him—frequently not knowing whether this is what he needs, or just the opposite.

The fact that doctors have been unable to control my husband's type of diabetes has in no way diminished our faith in them. They have often gone far beyond the call of duty in giving him extra-special care and attention in emergencies, exerting superhuman efforts to pull him through one crisis after another.

Of the two major complications we had been warned about, we were far more worried about the loss of a limb than loss of sight. Russell seemed to be forever dropping something on his feet and toes, or falling and injuring them, during his black-outs.

But the truth was that between the hospital interludes we were preoccupied with something far more important to us than the inconveniences of diabetes—and that was the sheer joy of living and working together. I would have followed Russell anywhere, and over the years I did—from Tahiti to Timbuktu, from Pago Pago to the Australian outback, from Bora Bora to Bali, Beirut, and Budapest, and around the world a few times.

And always with his cameras over his shoulders and the insulin and needles in his bag. With his cameras and my typewriter we had worked our way through college; with his enthusiasm for living life to its fullest and his adventurous spirit we had continued working our way through life, fulfilling many of the ardent hopes of youth.

Fortunately, our photojournalistic careers had brought us a certain amount of recognition that kept us in high spirits.

Russell was as much married to his cameras as he was to me; sometimes, it seemed to me, a lot more so. When he said he didn't intend to let his disease run his life, he meant exactly that.

The Dream

He might not always be able to control it, but it certainly would never control him. Between my husband and God—and a few empathetic editors—we were living a full and good life with excitement and challenges, working out of improvised darkrooms in the unlikeliest places, from the tiny bathroom of a New York slum apartment to a Park Avenue penthouse, in shower stalls, ships' galleys, hotels, and thatched huts around the world.

Russell even managed to enrich his life during his hospital stays. Nurses and doctors have walked into his room to find him practicing the cello and tying trout flies. While recuperating, he has repaired doctors' and nurses' cameras, radio and television sets, and anything else that needed fixing. In Palm Springs one of his doctors became an expert photographer after bedside instruction from Russell.

During one of Russell's month-long interludes at Passavant Hospital in Chicago (which for years was our second home), he enrolled in and completed a six-month course in electronics. He received his diploma and was offered a job teaching at the school (he turned it down), while doctors pondered how to control his blood sugar. His electronics instruction kits kept his mind and his hands occupied and amused his doctors and nurses. "Now what are you building?" they would ask, viewing the clutter on his bed. "Just a gadget," he would say.

From this beginning in a hospital room he learned to combine electronics with photography, make his own sound tracks,

9

and produce commercial and educational films on subjects rang-
ing from *The Psychic Life of the Aborigines* to *How to Play the
Violin.*

Life has a way of making certain misfortunes of the past pay
extra dividends for the future. Each time I view the clutter on
our front patio, my mind flashes back to those bedside scenes at
Passavant and I think how lucky we are that he learned to make
all those gadgets. For the miracle of the hummingbird really
began then.

CHAPTER TWO

The Reality

In the spring of 1968 we had moved to California on a new job assignment, covering the glamorous and exciting world of entertainment. Russell's daily dependence on insulin had not diminished his enthusiasm for life or his confidence in the future. His eyes were still good, his photographic work still in demand. His pictures of Hollywood movie stars graced many magazine covers. We had found a house that seemed meant for us, with ample space for working quarters—photography studio, darkroom, and offices, on one level, and living quarters on another. Life was beautiful.

One day, without telling me, Russell asked my assistant, Vera, to find an eye specialist, make an appointment, and drive him to the doctor's office—he couldn't see well enough to drive himself.

He didn't tell me at first because he hoped the eye problem might be only temporary, something that could be fixed. But it wasn't. Then he realized he had to tell me.

"It's finally gotten to my eyes," he said. "I'm losing my sight."

"Both eyes?"

"Both eyes."

He was quiet a minute. Then he said, "I'd rather lose a leg than my eyes. That's one thing I can't take."

There was a huskiness in his voice, a cracking, dry-in-the-throat sound I had never heard before. I tried to think of something to say. I was as dry in the throat as he was.

In the deafening silence, each of us knew what the other was thinking, what we were sharing inside: the mental picture of his older sister Carmel in her last stages of progressive diabetic retinopathy, culminating in total blindness. (Diabetic retinopathy, in lay terms, is massive hemorrhaging of the blood vessels in the eyes, and is usually considered irreversible.) Memories of the tears that poured from her vacant, staring, unseeing eyes when we went to visit her. Then her sudden tragic death from a fall—but a death that mercifully released her from a world of darkness in which she was almost completely helpless.

Carmel had also been a brittle diabetic and, like Russell, instead of yielding to her affliction, she had turned it into a self-help opportunity. She went back to college, got a master's degree in nutrition, and became chief dietician at a hospital in Indianapolis. With her expertise she was better able to regulate her insulin and diet regimen than Russell was, and thus had fewer complications. When they did occur she was in a convenient spot for emergency medical care and a hospital bed. She was in fairly good control of her disease—and her life—until the blindness struck. Once it started, it progressed rapidly. And so did her deterioration, physically and mentally.

Russell broke the silence by saying quietly, "I'm not going through what Carmel went through."

"Doctors must know more about it now than when it happened to Carmel," I said. "Besides, remember, she was fifteen years older than you."

"That has nothing to do with it," he said. "When diabetes gets to your eyes, you're finished. Especially if you're a photographer. It's like a violin player losing his fingers."

All I could think at that moment was: We're too young for this to happen to us. He was barely fifty—young by average life standards. But a diabetic's life is different. We had been lucky so far; he had outlived by many years the doctor who gave him five years to live. Maybe the eye doctor was wrong, too.

But the next day we called a real estate agent and put a FOR SALE sign on our house.

We sold our house and bought a smaller one in Palm

Springs where Russell could get around more easily. I could commute to Hollywood to cover the entertainment world for my syndicated newspaper column. We began a frantic search for anything in medical science that might save Russell's sight. The only hope, we were told, was the laser beam operation, which in 1968 was still comparatively new, unproved, and risky. The beam had to be operated with pinpoint accuracy to "shoot" the "bleeders"—cauterize the hemorrhaging blood vessels. If it missed, it could destroy other optic areas. If it hit, it would stop the bleeding but leave scar tissue in the areas treated. There was no guarantee that it would stop the hemorrhaging permanently or prevent other vessels from bleeding. We were warned that each time the eyes were "zapped" by the laser there would be some visual field loss; sufficient laser destroys some of the nerve pathways; too many "zappings" might do more harm than good; any sight rceovery from the treatments might last only a few months, at best a few years.

Russell had his first laser beam operation at one of the most famous eye centers in the country. Unfortunately, his "bleeders" were too close to the optic nerve. The doctor shot all around them, never did hit the hemorrhaging vessels, and destroyed the vision in other areas, with the result that Russell came out of that hospital almost completely blind in one eye.

When I picked him up at the hospital, he had a black eye-patch over each eye. I remember distinctly the shock of seeing

14

those patches for the first time, not knowing that I would soon be seeing them regularly.

But more shocking was the change in my husband. The operation had been terribly painful and he was still in some pain, but he had endured physical pain before, many times, during previous diabetic complications, without flinching. This time discouragement and utter despair seemed to tear at him as he fumblingly gripped my arm and let me lead him to the car. He was no longer cheerfully in control of his life. He was helpless and dependent on someone else, which for him was intolerable and devastating. I remember thinking that all our years of living with diabetes were nothing compared with this. I suddenly knew why blindness had destroyed Carmel emotionally and why Russell had said he wouldn't go through what she had gone through.

We knew, of course, that when the eye patches came off he would still have some sight, but it would be only a matter of time until the inevitable darkness.

Actually, it was five years between the onset of blindness and the full realization that he could no longer see.

During those years he learned to adjust to his diminishing eyesight. Though he could no longer see well enough to go out on photographic assignments, he managed to carry on a small business in photocopying and color processing in the darkroom he had built in our garage. His mind and his hands were still busy. His confidence gradually returned—except when the eye hemorrhaging started again. Fortunately, soon after his first experience with the laser beam, he was accepted as a patient by Dr. Paul C. Wetzig, a pioneer in the use of the laser for photo-coagulation of the eyes, and head of the Colorado Springs Eye Clinic, a leading treatment center for the diabetic blind. Each time Russell came back from Colorado he could still see. He wasn't yet like Carmel.

Then he developed cataracts in both eyes, requiring immediate surgery and adding to the complication of diabetic retinopathy. For a while our life was a succession of black eye patches. On and off. In and out of the hospital in Palm Springs or Colorado.

I cannot recall precisely which eye patch it was—there had been so many—or exactly why this one was different from the others. But I remember clearly driving home from the hospital with knots in my stomach, and Gogi, our little brown poodle, standing up on the seat between us and licking at the eye patch.

"Down, Gogi! We don't need any more catastrophes in the family," I said.

I was thinking of the imminent possibility of an automobile accident. I had taken driving lessons from a number of instructors who, in turn, had told me to forget it. I was not constitutionally suited to driving. But Russell could no longer see the traffic signals. The last time he had tried to drive he had almost sideswiped a truck on the Palm Springs to Los Angeles freeway. I had had to take over the wheel. It was a terrifying experience for both of us. I finally got the car turned around and headed home.

There had been other drives home from the hospital over the same road, and there would be many more. But for some reason that I can't explain I knew that this one was the beginning of the end of our world as it had been.

Encroaching blindness is one thing; the final reality is quite another. After living for five years with his gradual loss of sight and getting accustomed to the idea, I assumed we were reasonably well prepared for the approaching moment of truth. We were not, and I doubt if anyone ever is.

Quite simply, it suddenly dawned on me that Russell really couldn't see anymore.

Otherwise it was a glorious day and I remember it as though it were only yesterday. It was a day that sparkled with the freshness of springtime on the desert: jacaranda trees in bloom with ethereal clusters of lacy lavender, flowering oleanders and circus-striped giant petunias, flaming beds of nasturtiums and bushes of Cape honeysuckle, blanketed fields of deep purple desert verbena.

All around us the shadow-boxed, craggy San Jacinto Mountains seemed so close you could reach out and touch them. Their distant peaks, coiffed with a mid-April snowfall, glistened in the dazzling sunlight.

"Look! There's still snow on the mountains," I said.

"Is there?"

Hesitantly I asked, "Can you see it?"

He turned his head, lifted the eye patch, and squinted. He said nothing.

"The petunias are *really* blooming *madly* this year."

"Are they?"

"I've never seen so much verbena before. Miles of it.   . ."

Babble, babble. I was trying to drown out the clamor of realization. I remember thinking to myself: *Anyone who can't see all these huge blobs of color has got to be*—I couldn't face the word.

That was part of the trouble. I had never really accepted the medical prognosis. Not that I doubted it—but some facts of life take a long time to sink in. This one had been cushioned by an emotional shock absorber that said: *Close your eyes. Shut it out. Think about it tomorrow or next week or next year. Not now. You can't do anything about it anyway (more than you are already doing), so don't think about it and maybe it will go away.*

But it didn't go away.

"Gogi, I guess we'll have to learn to put up with our new chauffeur," Russell said with a bleak smile, his only one on that long ride home.

"I'm doing okay," I said cheerfully. But my insides were shredded. With my twenty-twenty vision I looked more closely at all the beauty around us, trying to drink it all in as though seeing it for the first and last time, trying to imagine what it would be like for him never to see again the mountains and trees and flowers that he loved.

He patted Gogi and said, "And we're going to dye you white, little poodle, so I can see you better. How would you like being a Seeing Eye dog?"

Gogi, whose real name was Gauguin, was a chocolate-brown French poodle (*caniche*) of aristocratic descent (Piperscroft), eleven years old and the joy of our life, especially Russell's. They were inseparable.

I managed to get us home safely, with husband, eye patch, and poodle intact. I remember Russell's words as he reached over to feel the furry softness beside him in bed. "It's all right, Gogi. Tomorrow we'll go for a run in the sand dunes." That was a tomorrow that never came.

During the next few months I learned to say casually, "Here I am." And to cough or rattle papers or make a noise to let Russell know where I was. I learned to pull the vacuum sweeper out of the way so he wouldn't stumble over it, to push the mushroom stools under the coffee table and the garden hose under the bougainvillea bush.

Then Gogi got sick. I carried him to the hospital in my arms minutes after I put Russell on the plane to Colorado for another laser beam operation.

19

We talked on the phone each day to exchange medical progress reports. On the fifth day our veterinarian said Gogi was better and I could bring him home the next day. Russell was elated at this news and I was encouraged by his. The doctor had told him he could come home tomorrow.

The telephone rang at eight o'clock the next morning.

"I'm sorry to have to tell you . . ." the vet said.

A few hours later I met Russell at the airport. We went home and together we built a small wooden chest, lined it with Gogi's blankets, sweaters, and toys, covered him with his red and green hand-knitted Christmas coat, and buried him under the pomegranate tree in a shady corner of our back patio. We planted a rosebush at his feet and drank a toast to him with a split of champagne.

The next day I noticed that the redwood gate to our back patio was wide open. It was never left open.

"Why is the gate open?" I asked.

"I opened it," Russell said.

"Why?"

"Because if Gogi comes back, he'll need a way to get in."

He was perfectly serious, and it worried me. Losing Gogi on top of everything else was too much for him, I thought.

A mourning dove walked through the open gate, uttered three mournful coos, stood a moment beside our geranium bed eyeing us quizzically, then soared up and perched on a telephone wire, still cooing.

The Reality

There had always been birds around our house—mourning doves, mockingbirds, finches, swallows, sparrows, and wild canaries. We had admired their beauty and song as they soared high above us, flitting among the topmost fronds of our towering palm trees. But we had no special rapport with them. They had usually kept their distance as long as we had had Gogi.

It was another spring and the blue periwinkle had grown over Gogi's grave when the little red hummer came.

CHAPTER THREE

The First Hummer

The transition from the world of the sighted to the sightless was slow, at times buoyed by unexpected glimmers of good vision. "Now I can see you," he would say. "I can't see your face but I know you're there. I can see an image. . . ."

There were bedridden weeks of darkness, then the stumbling, groping adjustment to *feeling* his way around the house and yard.

Inevitably, he was confronted with options such as Braille, white-tipped canes, a Seeing Eye dog, a "rehabilitation" or "retraining" program in which he could enroll and learn another trade.

Russell rejected all of them. When well-meaning friends mentioned one or the other he recoiled in stony silence, or, if I made the suggestion, he lashed out at me.

"Why don't we get a Seeing Eye dog now that we don't have Gogi?" I asked him one day.

"I am not going to depend on a dog to lead me around," he said. "I can learn to get around by myself."

I did not repeat the question.

In the earlier stages of his sight loss several good friends and members of his family had discreetly broached the possibilities of learning Braille and enrolling in a rehabilitation program. With their help, but without his knowing it, I had investigated some of these possibilities.

I might as well have saved my time and energy. He bristled at the slightest hint of them.

"If I lose my sight altogether, then I'll have time to learn Braille. I don't want to hear any more about it," he informed me.

I had to caution people not to mention the word in his presence.

As for enrolling in a rehabilitation program, he was equally adamant.

"Why are you so opposed to it?" I asked. "Some of those programs are very good. They train you for different jobs. They find jobs for people who can't see. Why don't you at least think about it?"

"Look," he said, " I have thought about it. And I am completely against it. I don't need to be trained for another job. All I need to do is figure out a way to continue doing what I already know how to do and like to do. Photography is the only thing I have ever been interested in doing, the only thing I have ever done. I'll admit that not being able to see is very inconvenient at times. But I'll figure out something to do. Just give me a lttle time."

At one point he enrolled in a typing course at our local College of the Desert. A friend who was a student there drove him to classes three times a week—while he was still able to see the letters on the keyboard.

The course was interrupted by more eye hemorrhaging and another trip to Colorado for the laser beam. His recovery periods from those treatments varied, from a few days to a few weeks to a few months of intermittent blurred vision, no vision, or able-to-see-better vision. After his recovery on this occasion, he no longer went to his typing classes. I didn't mention it for some time. Then one day I asked casually, "What happened to your typing classes?"

"I gave them up," he said.

"Why?"

"I'll tell you why." There was a defiance in his tone that startled me. "I started that typing course with the wrong attitude, a defeatist attitude."

"What do you mean?"

"I only did it because I was thinking of something I could do without sight. There are two things you can do without being able to see," he said. "You can play the piano and you can type. You don't need to look at the keyboard to play the piano; you don't have to look at the letters on a typewriter to type. I was trying to think of something I could do when I couldn't see to make pictures anymore. Playing the piano would be more fun, but learning to use a typewriter would be more practical—if I lost my sight altogether. I was thinking, when this happens, then I'll have something to fall back on."

"So what's wrong with that? Isn't it better to be prepared— just in case?" I said.

"It's absolutely wrong. It's a defeatist attitude. It means you're giving up, accepting something that might never happen. It just hit me one day while I was sitting there in that typing class. I thought to myself: What am I doing here? Why am I taking a typing course? The only reason was that I was already figuring on losing my sight. I went into it thinking I could learn something I could use when I couldn't see. That's the wrong reason for taking a typing course, or any other course. I'll have plenty of time to learn to type after I lose my sight—*if* I lose it. But maybe I'm not going to lose it. Why have this defeatist attitude? Why keep thinking and planning on losing my sight when maybe I won't? If I keep thinking I'm going to, then I will. You have to tell yourself you're *not* going to."

He ended his little lecture by telling me that everyone (wife included) was wrong to try to push him into "aids to the blind" programs before he was ready.

"I'm not giving up yet. When I'm ready for Braille or a

Seeing Eye dog or a typing course, I'll let you know," he said.

He had a similar attitude toward using canes, or "walking sticks," as he preferred to call them.

He wouldn't have dreamed of buying one for himself, but friends began to bring him handsome, exotically decorative canes from faraway places. At least they were not white-tipped. One was a flashy red-and-yellow-striped and beaded stick from Africa that looked like a miniature barber pole and would have stopped traffic a mile away.

At first he seemed to enjoy the walking sticks as a novelty. He even used them on a few of his early excursions around the neighborhood when he was learning his way on foot.

Then one day I caught him going toward our bedroom closet with an armload of his walking sticks.

"What are you doing with those things?"

"I'm hiding them."

"Why?"

"I don't need them. I'm not going to be dependent on them."

I retrieved the African barber-pole stick to hang in my study. He tucked the others away in the closet, where they have reposed ever since.

Then there was the day he threw away his dark glasses. He had never worn dark glasses just because it was the chic thing to do. He wouldn't wear them even to keep the sun out of his eyes when he should have. Wearing dark glasses was as repugnant to him as wearing an ascot instead of a tie.

But when his eye problems started, he bought a pair of dark glasses and wore them for several weeks. One day I found a pair of dark glasses in the wastebasket and asked, "Are these your glasses?"

"Yes."

"What are they doing here?"

"I don't want them."

"Why not?"

"I was only using them to hide my eyes," he said. "That's why most blind people wear dark glasses, so other people can't see their eyes. Blind people sit and stare into space. It's easier to sit and stare if you're wearing dark glasses and no one can see you. You start drifting off. It's no good for you mentally. That's what happened to Carmel: sitting and staring into space. I'm not going to be like that. If you turn and look at people while they're talking, it makes you use your eyes, it *makes* you *think*, it makes *them* think you see better than you do."

So his dark glasses went the way of his walking sticks—out of his life.

For a while Russell preferred risking his life on my bicycle to asking me to drive him anywhere. Then he had to give up the bicycle, too. He resigned himself to my chauffeuring, but only when it was too far to walk and there was no one else around to drive him.

Such were the immediate, day-to-day, basic necessities of coping with realities. He learned and adjusted quickly, without complaint, to the touch-and-feel world around him. He accepted his loss of sight as an inconvenience but not a handicap. As long as he could tell light from dark, he refused to believe he couldn't see. He clung to the hope that his eyes would improve.

And for a long time he had faith in himself, in his ability to figure out a way, as he always put it, of continuing in the work he loved doing.

This happened to be something more than a simple love affair. In realistic terms, Russell's photography had also helped pay the bills. For a while people had brought him odd jobs that he could do in the darkroom, but then they stopped coming, the telephone stopped ringing.

We passed through a time of anguish: the period of having him declared "legally blind," the hassles with Social Security, Medicare, and the assorted bureaucrats who dole out the "disability pension" for the blind, a monthly stipend that would pay about a third of the cost of his round-trip plane ticket to Colorado. We had always associated these things with the aged and infirm.

For a man barely into his fifties, still in his prime professionally, this experience started the breakdown in his spirit.

Years earlier he could have qualified as "legally blind" (a technicality requiring a written declaration from three doctors, specialists in ophthalmology, that a patient has less than 10 percent vision) and thus have been eligible for government assistance. To do so was simply unthinkable, for both of us, and in any case it seemed a distant prospect.

But it's the today, here, and now that count when the bills come due. And there is no more crushing blow to a man's spirit and pride and independence than not to be able to shoulder his share of a financial burden. These are very personal matters, the kind usually glossed over in the how-to-cope books. Many people write about their problems as though they themselves are financially secure, and maybe they are. Many will argue interminably that money isn't important. Probably not, if you have plenty of it.

One morning Russell asked in a strangely urgent tone, "Would you mind driving me up to the camera shop?"

"Sure." I wondered what he would possibly need from the camera shop, since he was no longer in the photography business.

As we got in the car I noticed that the back seat was loaded with his cameras and photographic equipment.

"What are you doing with them?"

"I'm going to sell them."

I didn't have to ask him why. "I don't need them anymore and we can use the money," he said.

This was the finality I had dreaded. He was giving up as a photographer. He had been discouraged at having to give up his business, but to give up his cameras meant that he was giving up hope.

"Are you sure this is what you want to do?"

"It isn't what I want to do. It's what I have to do. I kept thinking my eyes might get better, but I guess they're not going to. So I have to face it."

He left the equipment in the camera store for the owner to sell.

From that day on, he began to have long spells of moodiness and despondency. I sometimes caught him doing the one thing he had said he would *never* do—sitting and staring into space. I knew what he was thinking: he was finished, washed up as a photographer, a has-been. He never admitted it in so many words, but it was written in the quiet despair of his voice, the stoop of his shoulders, the shuffling walk, the afternoon naps that grew longer and longer.

His smile had vanished, his enthusiasm was gone, he seemed to have lost all interest in even trying to figure out a way to do something, anything.

He was sitting and staring into space on our front patio one evening at dusk when I blurted out, a bit edgily, "*What* has happened to you?"

"What do you mean?"

"I mean, what's happened to your Pollyanna sunny-side-up? *You're* the one who's always preaching to *me* about looking on the bright side. Now it's my turn. Okay?"

"Okay." Then silence. Not a flicker of a smile.

"Don't you have anything to say?"

"Yes. I've been thinking."

"And what have you decided?"

"I've decided that we should sell the house and make a down payment on a motel," he said.

"What for?"

"I could manage a motel. I can see enough to do that. It would give us an income."

"You mean you would really sell this house?"

"I think we should," he said. "We could live in the motel. It would be a good investment. I could do the carpentry and repair work and be the manager. I could learn to do that. It would save us money and take all these mortgage payments off your shoulders. . . ."

So that's what was bothering him!

"Look," I said. "We are *not* selling this house. That's one point where I put my foot down. Emphatically. Okay?"

"But I have to figure out something I can do."

"You will. But we're not selling this house."

I had curtailed my commuting and traveling assignments; he could no longer be left alone. Our little Palm Springs house had become my working headquarters—as well as home. And we both loved it.

We could smell the charcoal coals burning in our barbecue. We were waiting for them to get hot enough to cook our hamburgers. Our orange tree was in bloom and the fragrance from its blossoms filled the air.

I got up and picked a lemon from our lemon tree, went inside, and fixed drinks and a tray of cheese snacks.

"Here, Glum Face, maybe this will cheer you up," I said, placing a gin and tonic in his hands.

"Oh, I'll be all right. . . . Maybe I should enroll in one of those training programs after all. . . ."

I swallowed the lump in my throat and cried, "Cheers!" I've got a better idea. We'll set up a lemonade stand in front of the house and sell homemade lemonade from our own homegrown lemon trees. I'll pick the lemons, you squeeze them. . . ."

"No, I'll pick and you squeeze. And we can save the lemon peels, slice them and freeze them, and sell them to martini drinkers. . . ."

No amount of banter could hide the truth: He was at his lowest ebb. And I wasn't far behind.

At that moment we heard a whirring of wings and a soft chic-chicing as a tiny bird zipped past us, then came to an abrupt stop in midair, spun around, and hovered in front of us, eyeing us quizzically, his wings beating so rapidly I could barely see them.

"It's a hummingbird," Russell said.

"How do *you* know?" He would have been hard put to see a pelican right in front of his nose.

"I can hear it. Now where did he go?"

"He's perched up in the orange tree looking at us. . . . Now he's coming back."

The little bird zoomed straight at Russell's head, put on his brakes a few inches in front of his face, and hung there as though suspended by an invisible thread, yo-yoing up and down, beating his wings and clickety-clacking noisily as Russell talked to him softly. "Hello, little hummingbird. What are you doing here? Where did you come from?"

The bird had a brilliant red head and throat that glittered like rubies in certain angles of the sunlight. His back was green.

"Now I see him," Russell said. "I can see red flashes and movement. . . . You're a pretty little redbird, come here little redbird. . . . I think he's trying to tell me something." The bird darted and dived up and down and around him, bzee-bzeeing in his ear and then spinning into a spectacular performance of aerial acrobatics, flashing his colors like jewels in a fireworks explosion.

It was the first time we had ever seen a hummingbird at close range.

"I didn't know hummingbirds were that beautiful," I said. "Did you?"

"No. I don't know anything about them. I don't remember even seeing a picture of a hummingbird," Russell said.

The little redbird was there all evening long, whirring

among the flowers and trees and oleander bushes, perching in the orange tree while we had our hamburgers.

"Are you hungry, little hummingbird? . . . I wonder what one feeds hummingbirds. Maybe we should put up a bird feeder," he said.

Later we scoured the neighborhood supermarkets until we found a hummingbird feeder in the pet food section. I read the label aloud:

"Deluxe Feeder. . . . Enjoy watching the tiniest, the quickest, most agile, most fascinating birds in creation. Fun for shut-ins, children, bird-watchers, camera bugs, everyone!"

"Shut-ins. That's for me!" Russell laughed, the first time in weeks.

The box contained diagrams and instructions on how to assemble the feeder, where to hang it (among flowering vines and shrubbery), what to feed the birds—a mixture of sugar water with a few drops of red food coloring.

There was also a brief summary of "Hummingbird Facts": They hover motionless, can fly backwards, consume half their weight in food daily, may fall into a state of suspended animation in order to conserve energy until food is available, may eat from your feeder as often as every fifteen minutes.

With this boxtop course in ornithology we bought five pounds of sugar and a bottle of red food coloring, hurried home, and put a pot of sugar water on to boil. While it cooled, Russell carefully assembled the feeder. He seemed to know instinctively how to do it. But he didn't much care for it when he had finished. "Plastic," he grumbled. "I can build a better one than this."

He filled the feeder and hung it on a branch of the orange tree.

The next morning before breakfast he was out on the front patio—not sitting and staring into space but standing beside the orange tree holding the feeder high in both hands against the bright sun, tipping it slowly to one side and then the other, moving it up and down, and all the while talking to the little red hummingbird as it hovered and followed the feeder.

After his second cup of coffee he announced, "I've got it figured out."

"What?"

"How to build a feeder. That one is no good. It's too flimsy and it draws the big birds."

He was right. The orioles and finches were freeloading off the hummingbird feeder. Russell spent most of the day shooing off the big birds, replenishing the sugar water, and building a new feeder. I watched this project, in its various stages, with consternation.

First I found him sitting in his chair on the back patio, outside his workshop, with a tonic bottle and a ball of heavy twine in his lap. He was patiently wrapping the twine around the bottle.

"What's that for?" I asked.

35

"It's my hummingbird feeder."

"But why the twine?"

"I'm going to paint it red."

I was still puzzled. "But why go to all that bother when the bottle will be filled with red sugar water?"

"This will look better. The glass is too shiny."

How that could possibly make any difference to a hungry hummingbird was beyond me, but Russell seemed to know what he was doing. In a little while I saw the freshly sprayed bottle lying on a newspaper in the sun to dry.

Then he called in to say, "Al [our next-door neighbor] is driving me to the hardware store. I need a few things." He came home with a paper sack in his arms and a few minutes later I found him melting a piece of glass tubing on our kitchen stove.

"This is the spout," he explained. "It has to be the right shape and size so the big birds can't get to it."

When he had finished melting the glass, he held an ice pick over the gas burner until it was red-hot, then proceeded to drill a hole in a small rubber tip, the kind used to cushion the legs of metal patio chairs. He fitted the tip over one end of the spout, inserted the other end of the spout into a rubber cork in the tonic bottle, then asked, "Do you have any red fingernail polish?"

"No. What do you need it for?"

"I have to paint the tip red, and real paint won't work on rubber."

I drove to the dime store and bought a bottle of red nail polish.

He painted the tip, held the red-twined bottle up for me to look at and said, "There! That's my hummingbird feeder. Now we'll see if it works."

Next he set up a three-pronged metal stand in the grassy center of our front patio.

"What's that for?"

"It's where I'm going to hang my hummingbird feeder," he said.

"But you're supposed to hang it near the flowers or trees or bushes where the birds are, not in the middle of nowhere, not in direct sunlight. That's what it says on the box the feeder came in."

"I don't care what the box says. *This* feeder didn't come in that box and this is the place where I want my feeder."

"Where'd you get the stand?"

"Out of my junk box. It's the bottom end of that Sun-God lamp you lugged home from Mexico. Don't you remember?"

Yes, I remembered. I had bought the lamp for him as an anniversary gift while I was on an assignment in Acapulco—on location with Rosalind Russell for one of her last movies. He had separated the lamp from its stand and attached the lamp itself to one of the walls of our back patio near a bougainvillea bush that I had given him for another anniversary (it had since grown into a canopy). Characteristically he had put the stand in his "junk box" for possible future use.

"I knew it would come in handy," he said. "See, I put this little metal crossbar on it to hang the feeder on."

I looked at his crossbar, a six-inch narrow slab of metal firmly atttached across the small round steel top of the lampstand to form a T-shaped arm.

"How did you do that?"

"I just drilled a hole and threaded it on."

"Wouldn't it be simpler to hang the feeder on a branch, or on one of our planter chains?" I asked. Besides all our trees and shrubbery, we had an abundance of brackets and chains under our tile eaves for hanging pots, planters, and wind chimes. There were plenty of natural and ready-made spots that would have been perfect for hanging a hummingbird feeder.

"I'll be able to see it better here," Russell said.

He removed the plastic feeder from the orange tree, went inside, and filled his tonic bottle with sugar water. As he returned to the lampstand the red hummingbird whirred around him, dive-bombing at the bottle and squawking furiously.

"That's all right, little redbird, you're going to be fed. See, you have a new feeder."

As soon as he hung he feeder on the lampstand, the hummingbird began plunging his long bill into the shiny red spout.

Russell stood by quietly, his head within inches of the tiny bird. Then he stepped back and said, "Well, it works."

In the days that followed, his moodiness disappeared. The change in him was more than a gradual improvement in his state of mind, more than a natural enthusiasm for a new "hobby."

Russell had never had a hobby per se. His work was his hobby. Now he began to act as if he was *working* at something again. He seemed driven, as if he had a secret goal beyond the simple pleasure of making hummingbird feeders for all our friends.

Everyone was fascinated with his feeders. He made them for birthday, anniversary, and Christmas gifts. Before long he had strung a necklace of his red-twined, red-tipped bottle feeders all the way from the shores of Santa Monica to northern Lake Michigan.

Inside each feeder bottle he tucked a neatly rolled slip of notepaper, carrying advice on "The Tender Loving Care and Feeding of Hummingbirds," along with his tried-and-tested sugar-water formula: one-third cup sugar, two-thirds cup water, two drops red food coloring.

One morning before breakfast, and with a perfectly straight face he asked me, "Would you like a gin and tonic?"

"What?"

He laughed and patted my shoulder. "I need some more bottles."

"Why don't you go into business? Sell them instead of giving them away." I was only half joking. Several friends had suggested the idea. He always shrugged it off.

I was glad he had found something to occupy his time, his mind, and his hands. But I was more intrigued with what was happening on our front patio. He no longer sat in his big yellow chair, his eyes vacant and motionless. They were now focused on the lampstand and his hummingbird feeder. They moved around, up and down and sideways, as he turned his head, trying to catch the movement and colors and sound of hummingbirds buzzing around him and at the feeder.

More hummingbirds began coming, at first two or three, then five or six, soon at least a dozen that we could count. He learned to recognize several of them by their distinctive whirring and buzzing, by their behavior patterns, colors, and highly vocal trademarks—from a soft chik-chik-chik to shrill, squeaky notes, to a beetle- or locust-like drone and the noisy clickety-clack squawking, as Russell called it, of his first Little Redbird. This one remained his favorite. He could recognize it at once with its wing buzzing, its flashes of red, its castanet claps in his ear when the feeder was empty.

He became totally absorbed in the activity at his hummingbird feeder. He would sit watching it for a while, then he would walk over and move the lampstand a few inches one way or another, turning the feeder to a different angle. Often he would tie a nasturtium or hibiscus blossom on the spout.

That, I thought, was very peculiar. If the birds wanted real nectar, all they had to do was go smorgasbording around our house. They obviously did not need flowers to lure them to the feeder.

"But it's prettier, it looks better," Russell explained. "Besides, I'm trying to figure something out."

Whatever it was, I knew he would tell me when he was ready and not before.

CHAPTER FOUR

We Become Hummingbirders

Russell came shuffling across the patio one evening with a camera and tripod in hand.

"Where did you get the camera?"

"It's my Nikon. The one I bought in Hong Kong, remember?"

I thought he had sold all his photographic equipment. He had in fact sold most of it—his movie cameras and projectors, his expensive Hasselblad outfit of viewfinders, lenses, and bellows (he was one of the first to buy and start using the Hasselblad "system"), his various Rolleiflex and Speed Graphic cameras.

"I kept this and one of my Speed Graphics just in case I might be able to use them someday," he said. "You never know."

He placed the Nikon on the tripod near the feeder, wrapped

42

a piece of white cloth—from an old pillowcase—around one end of a long, slender piece of wood that he called his "focusing stick," and said to me, "Now, would you like to help me? Just hold the stick there. Like this."

"What are you trying to do?"

"Get a picture of that hummingbird."

The hummingbirds moved so swiftly that I secretly doubted they could be photographed at all—I could not recall seeing any photographs of hummingbirds anywhere—but there was no harm in humoring him.

He clamped his hand over mine at the white end of the stick, and moved it slowly around and up and down within inches of the red-tipped feeder spout, explaining, "This is where I want the hummingbird, where the white spot is. I can see that in the viewfinder."

He moved back to the camera and I moved to the other end of the five-foot focusing stick. My shoulders ached as I held the thing, trying to keep it steady, while he searched in the viewfinder, trying to find the white spot. He finally did. I put the focusing stick down by the big redwood petunia pot where he could find it if he needed it, and then we waited for the little redbird to begin performing where the white spot had been.

As I had suspected, it wasn't all that simple to get a picture of a hummingbird.

At first he used a cable-cord system of triggering the shutter

—extension cords from camera and strobe lights with a rubber bulb at one end that he held in his hands and pressed on cue from me.

When a hummingbird was at the feeder, in the right position in front of the camera, I would say, "There!" and he would press the rubber bulb and ask, "Did the light go off?"

Sometimes it did and sometimes it didn't.

I also tried to help clue him in on the colors. "There's a purple one." Or green, or red.

He was especially anxious to catch that first little redbird in his camera.

Other hummingbirds came and flashed the same brilliance of red.

"There he is," I would say.

"No it isn't."

"How do you know?"

"I can tell. He's different from the others."

Photographically it didn't matter. All the shots turned out the same in the darkroom—blanks, blurs, and no birds. During his first week of shooting he wasted several rolls of film, getting nothing but wing tips, the end of a tail, part of a beak, or, more often, blank film.

After developing each roll of film, he would report, "Well, I'm not having any luck yet. I'll have to try something else." After one roll, he announced, "I'm making progress. I got one good hand and two finches on this one." He held the roll of film up against the light for me to look at. Out of ten exposures he had seven blanks and blurs, a shot of his own hands as he accidentally tripped the shutter, and two shots of a finch at the feeder.

"At least you got a bird," I said. It was the first picture he had taken of anything in months.

"The hummingbirds are too fast. By the time the shutter goes off they're three blocks down the street. I'll figure out something. . . ."

He began poring over strange pieces of equipment that suddenly mushroomed on our front patio.

When his friends dropped by to offer him a ride uptown, as they often did, most often now he accepted—eagerly. For a while he had been hesitant about imposing on anyone. Now it seemed neccessary for him to make frequent trips to the hardware and dime stores, the Radio Shack, the camera and photo supply shops. He was also beating a path between his workshop, which he had built onto the garage back of the house, and our front patio, which was beginning to look as though a cyclone had hit it.

"Why is all this stuff necessary?" I asked.

"I'm building a bird shooter. I think I've got it all figured out how to catch my hummingbirds. I'm fixing it so they'll take their own pictures."

"That's nice," I said skeptically. "Have you told the birds about it?"

45

"Just wait till I get it all working. See—look at this." He held up a small metal box, moved his finger in front of it, and it made a clicking sound.

"What's that?"

"It's a door opener. I built it. I think it's going to work fine when I get everything working in synch."

"What does a door opener have to do with a bird shooter?"

"It's the relay that sets off the camera," he explained. "You know those electric-eye doors you walk through at the grocery store? That's where I got the idea. You walk through a beam and the door opens. I got to thinking about it and I decided I could do the same thing with the hummingbirds and the camera.

"It's all done with electronics. When a hummingbird flies in front of the camera, it will break the beam and trip the camera shutter and set off the lights at the same time. Maybe I'll start getting pictures—I hope."

He moved his forefinger in front of his door-opener gadget again to demonstrate, smiled as he listened to the clicking sounds, and said excitedly, "See, it's working!"

"How?"

"Don't you understand? You see my finger here? This is the hummingbird. He flies in front of the camera and breaks the beam and it makes the relay click."

"But this isn't the camera. . . ."

"No, dopey, it's the cell, the seeing eye that makes the bird shooter work."

We Become Hummingbirders

On the very first evening that he got his seeing eye to work, he also got pictures of hummingbirds for the first time.

Not good ones, to be sure, but at least they were hummingbirds and not finches. The images were often out of focus, off center, or too small to print but Russell remained unperturbed at what came out of his developing tank and calmly set about improving his seeing eye, improvising and building new equipment. His original "door opener," he found, was not sensitive enough—the beam was too wide. He redesigned it, using a phototransistor to narrow the beam. He built or redesigned his own strobe lights to fire faster than the commercial ones available—or those he could afford. He encased the power supply for his strobes in a big black-box container that he made from a discarded air conditioner. This unsightly thing occupied a prominent corner of our patio.

Our patio tables were cluttered with hammers, screwdrivers, pliers, nails; our yard was a tangled maze of electrical cords and wiring that ran between various lights, cameras, battery boxes, and bird feeder, and to plugs both inside and outside the house.

I learned to accept his complicated explanations without comprehending them: "I'm redesigning the circuitry. He's breaking the beam but it's not going off. . . . I'm trying to build a plunger to set this to run off of six volts."

"Just don't get yourself electrocuted," I said frequently. Each time I heard a crash I thought he had. I would run out of the house and find him picking himself up from a tumble over a lawn sprinkler or patio stool—something he had forgotten was there and didn't see. He never stumbled over his own equipment. He knew exactly where everything was because he had just put it there. I had strict orders to move nothing.

At one point I counted nine pieces of major equipment on the front lawn, all indispensable for his seeing-eye bird shooting, and all homemade by him except camera and tripods. Even these he had changed, modified, designed, or adapted to suit his needs.

In developing and perfecting his complicated method of shooting hummingbird pictures, he had to solve certain problems that would not have presented themselves to a person of sufficient financial means and eyesight. For example, after he had figured out most of the mechanical, technical, engineering, and electronics problems and was convinced that the seeing eye would work satisfactorily, he had to face a different kind of obstacle: his camera. He was working with his 35 mm Nikon, and it was catching the hummingbirds all right but the images were still too small for Russell to see to print them. We invested in a new camera, a Mamiya RB67 that would give him a larger image in the viewfinder and on film—2¼ x 2¾, about six times larger than the 35 mm film. He also adapted a lens from his old Speed Graphic to the Mamiya because the Speed Graphic lens was easier to trip with his solenoid.

The new camera was much heavier than the old one, more cumbersome to move around on a tripod, so Russell designed a movable arm for the tripod and found a machinist friend to build it for him. Thus he could simply turn a knob and slide the camera back and forth to focus on the bird feeder without moving the tripod. He also learned a few tricks of the machinist's trade and began turning out intricate parts for lens carriers and holders on a metal lathe in his own workshop.

Some of them would have been difficult to make even for someone with perfect vision. "How do you do it?" I asked him one day.

"I use my other senses," he replied. "If I'm trying to touch a red-hot soldering iron on a pinpoint, I know it when I'm too close. By the *feel*. Of the heat. If it burns, then I *know* I'm too close."

Months passed. I wondered when, if ever, he would get all of his bird-shooting equipment working in synch—shutters clicking, lights popping, buzzers buzzing, and birds hovering where he wanted them, all at the same time.

There always seemed to be something else he had to figure out before printing any hummingbird pictures. When he couldn't find a certain type of camera cord to fit his solenoid, he made a new electrical connection by soldering together two nails and a piece of wiring. He kept experimenting with his "power suppliers" to get the voltage he needed, and with different bird-shooting backgrounds for color and lighting effects.

He made his first background from a piece of plywood, which he painted yellow on one side and red on the other and

49

mounted on a tripod near the feeder. This proved to be too cumbersome, so he bought a three-by-five-foot window blind at the dime store, sprayed it yellow, and mounted it on a cross-board that he built atop his tripod. The bright yellow was easier for him to see for focusing or adjusting as he rolled the window shade up or down. He piled a stack of bricks on the patio beside the orange tree to anchor the blind in the strong winds we often have in Palm Springs, and also to hold down the plastic covers for his cameras and other equipment.

Once I found him at his workbench dismantling a bright red toy fire engine that still had the $1.98 price tag on it from Woolworth's.

"What are you doing with *that?*"

"I'm taking the wheels off to make a roller for my bird prints," he explained. "I sold my other roller, but the one I'm building will be just as good when I get these wheels on it."

He also had to build new developing trays, an enlarging stand, and other darkroom equipment to replace items he had sold.

"When do you think you might start printing?" I asked.

"When I'm ready. And when I get anything good enough to print. Printing color pictures is expensive," he reminded me. "I can't afford to waste paper. My exposures must be off. I'm not catching the colors of the birds."

"But you're catching the birds. They look fine to me. Why don't you print just one or two?"

"I'm going to. But not yet."

One day I glanced out the window of my study, which overlooks the front patio, and I saw Russell treading gingerly among all his equipment. This in itself wasn't unusual, but he was carrying an old beat-up black umbrella over his head.

I sprinted outside to make my usual inquiry.

"I thought it might rain," he quipped. Then he explained, "It's my light reflector. See, I sprayed it white inside. That's to give a soft, diffused lighting on the hummingbirds. Makes the light bounce better. I'm trying to catch those colors. "

He set the umbrella down beside his bird feeder and seeing-eye setup, and tipped it around and from side to side to show me how it worked, explaining, "Now, if I want the reflection from this angle . . ."

"Where did you get the umbrella?"

"In my junk box." As if reading my thoughts, he added, "I know it looks like a mess. If we had a fortune I could hire an electronics firm to do all of this for me and it would be very professional-looking. I could buy a good light reflector for twenty-five or thirty dollars, but this old umbrella works fine. Like my strobes—they're not the fanciest things in the world, but they work. And my solenoid. It only cost me five or six dollars at the most, and a scientist would be horrified by how I made it. But it works."

Six months passed before Russell made his first color print. During all of this time, except for one period of eye hemorrhaging and another trip to the hospital in Colorado Springs, he remained in high spirits, working slowly, patiently, but with unflagging determination toward perfecting his seeing-eye equipment. He was completely absorbed in the project, like a man possessed. He no longer sat and stared into space.

Equally important, he no longer rejected the reality that he was indeed blind. It is one thing to know the facts and another to accept them. Russell's acceptance came with the hummingbirds and his first vocalization of the word *blind*, a word that neither of us had been able to use earlier.

He had finally forced himself to say the word late one night at the Los Angeles International Airport upon returning from Colorado. Due to a mix-up in plane schedules—or a communications gap between us—I was not there to meet him when the plane landed. Although I would have preferred to go with him on these trips, we could not afford two round-trip fares, and it wasn't really necessary. The airline stewardesses took good care of him. On this occasion the stewardess had left him in a telephone booth trying to find out where his wife was. I was still in Palm Springs. He tried to reach Vera, my assistant, who lived in Los Angeles, but couldn't remember her number— and couldn't see well enough to find it in the phone directory. After fumbling through the pages, exasperated and discouraged, he dialed the operator and said, "I'm sorry to bother you but— I'm blind. I wonder if you could help me find a number."

She did, and Vera picked him up at the airport, then put

him on a plane the next day for Palm Springs. When I met him, a smiling stewardess held him securely by the arm, having just snatched him from nearly walking into the airplane propeller.

"Honey, let's face it," he said, "you've got a blind husband."

He said it with no trace of hopelessness or despair. And somehow, having once admitted it openly, his faith in himself seemed stronger than it had ever been. In his earlier rejection of Braille, rehabilitation courses, canes, and a Seeing Eye dog, his self-confidence had been based mostly on a *denial* rather than on acceptance of reality. He had refused to become dependent on any "aids to the *blind*" because the fact was repugnant to him.

The hummingbirds helped him over that hurdle by giving him a goal to work toward, a greater challenge than anything he had ever attempted even when he had normal vision; and by making him accept his loss of sight as a reality but not an insurmountable handicap.

Once, while he was struggling over a particularly difficult electronics problem, he told me, "I'll get it eventually. Not being able to see, it takes me ten times longer to do things. But I still usually get them done. Lots of people have problems. Mine happens to be an eye problem. So I see in other ways, with my hands and feet and my ears." He looked up at me with a grin. "I see some things better than you do."

"That's for sure."

I would never ask *him* to help *me* find something I had lost or misplaced; after all, I'm the one who can see. But one morning I was tearing the place apart trying to find my reading glasses. I can't work without them. He said calmly, "Just stop and *think*. Now, you want me to find them for you? Here they are."

He reached under the cushion of the blue chair in front of the fireplace where the night before I had fallen asleep reading, and sure enough—there were my glasses. This became a familiar pattern. He seemed to have an intuitive awareness of where mislaid objects could be: books, car keys, juice squeezer, the lost-and-found trivia of daily living.

Whenever he dropped a tiny something or other and asked me to help him find it, as he often did, he was nearly always the first to say, "I've found it." He developed remarkable accuracy in his "touch-and-feel" system, as he called it.

After six months of his touch-and-feel building of bird-shooting and film-processing equipment, he came in the house one morning and announced, "Well, here they are. My first hummingbird prints. What do you think of them?" He spread out three color photos on the coffee table. They were small five-by-seven prints and not only beautiful but fascinating.

The photographs, enlarged to show the birds several times their actual size, revealed certain characteristics and flight positions that we could not see in watching the actual birds. One, a closeup of a hummingbird's head, which is no bigger than a dime, showed an elliptical pattern of faintly red feathers—and a huge eye in the center. One was a front view of a bird that looked as if he were standing on his tail with his tiny feet tucked in front of him. Another had his tail and wings spread out in a sideways barrel roll at the feeder.

But Russell was dissatisfied. "I'm not catching the colors," he complained. The most vivid colors were those of the flowers he tied to the feeder. He had other complaints, too. Some of the pictures were out of focus. Some of the birds' bills were cut off or their wings blurred. And a good many of his prints, of course, were simply bad prints, as might be expected—the result of his own mistakes in the color processing, his touch-and-feel system of experimenting with types of papers and chemicals, color film, water and chemical temperatures, timing, enlarging. Color photography is a complicated and specialized field, as those in the business know. Fortunately, Russell's many years of professional experience gave him an enormous advantage. He had a reputation as one of the best in the business. Even long after he began losing his sight he was still teaching other photographers to do color work. Most of them readily admitted he could make better color pictures half-blind than they could with perfect eyesight.

But bird photography was something different. It was a specialty in itself.

And so were hummingbirds, we were beginning to find out.

The only birds Russell had ever photographed before were the flamingos in Hialeah Park.

He Saw a Hummingbird

He didn't know that the odds against a photographer's catching a hummingbird on film were thirty to one. Almost every day he would come in with two or three more prints for me to look at. Then usually he would take them back to the "reject" pile in his studio. His stack of rejects was growing, but gradually so was the number of passable prints he left in the house.

Everyone who saw them was astonished—not only that Russell, who was considered a has-been, finished as a photographer because of his eyes, was making pictures, but that he was photographing hummingbirds. Most people simply didn't believe it. The usual reaction was, "But even people with twenty-twenty vision can't get pictures of hummingbirds."

Russell's stock answer was, "Nothing to it. I just set up the camera and the birds take their own pictures."

But he was secretly pleased at the interest the pictures were creating. And we were both impressed when an artist friend, John Morris, dropped by one day and liked one of the pictures so much that he wanted to buy it. Russell insisted on giving it to him.

John had given Russell a good many picture jobs, photographing him at work and making photocopies of his paintings for his gallery brochures.

"Did you know you're doing something that is very unusual?" John said. "If you can come up with enough prints that are as good as these, you should think about having an exhibit. This one, for example"—he picked up one of the photographs and

studied it closely—"it doesn't look like a photograph, it looks
like an abstract painting . . . like *Nude Descending the Stair-
case* . . . or something. . . ."

"That's one of my mistakes," Russell said. "One of the
strobes didn't go off."

"Some of an artist's best works are mistakes and accidents,"
John said. "So it's dark and shadowy, it looks more like a
silhouette than a hummingbird. Why don't you name it *Silhouette*? . . . And this one looks like a ballerina in tutu. It
should be named *Ballerina*."

Ballerina was the one I had picked as my favorite. It was a
bird flipped over like a feather duster against a background of
yellow pansies tied on the feeder (for color and composition);
and the camera had caught a small but distinct patch of purple
throat streamers on the bird. It was one of Russell's very first
prints and the only one he had yet that showed off a bird's
coloring halfway to his satisfaction, but he was about to toss it
in his basket of rejects because it was "too fuzzy."

John's enthusiasm was a great boost. And there were others.
I began taking some of the best prints to an art store to have
them framed, and each time I went to pick them up, the framer,
shop clerks, or customers would ask, "Are these for sale?"

My answer was always no.

I took them home and hung them in our dinette-den, which
Russell had recently usurped for his coffee-and-think shop, a
place where he spent hours (it had the best lighting in the

house) poring over electronics books, gadgetry, and bird-shooting problems—with a magnifying glass and a special jeweler's loupe, a small but powerful magnifier that fitted over one side of his eyeglasses like a monocle. As an added incentive for him, I promised to take down all of my floor-to-ceiling clown paintings and my cherished batik from a Balinese temple and rehang all the walls in hummingbird pictures just as fast as he could make them for me.

Neither of us had any thought of reactivating his career or embarking on a new one. With hummingbirds? We didn't consider ourselves even amateur ornithologists. We had never been on an Audubon bird walk. The hummingbirds were keeping Russell busy and giving him daily practice in exercising his eye muscles, moving his head and eyes back and forth, making him use all his wits and skills and sensory abilities to the utmost.

Our limited feeder-boxtop knowledge of hummingbirds did not detract from the pleasure of watching them or the challenge of photographing them. To begin with we identified them by names, as John Morris had suggested, according to various characteristics and behavior. One we called Flirty Bird because she acted like a flirt (though we couldn't tell one sex from another); one we named Freddy for Fred Astaire, a hummer whose coloring resembled black and white tie and tails; a purple-headed one we called Cassius because he perched arrogantly on a high twig in the orange tree and dive-bombed any other bird that came near the feeder.

Now and then someone would look at one of the pictures

and ask, "What species of hummingbird is it?" We didn't know there were different species. To us a hummingbird was a hummingbird. To tell the truth, Russell really didn't care beans about identifying the species. All he wanted was to get a picture that looked like a hummingbird.

But my curiosity was piqued. I went to my friendly bookstore proprietor and asked for the best book he had on hummingbirds. He had none, he said; he wished he did have; books on hummingbirds were rare, out of print, hard to find; he would scout around and try to find one for me. Meanwhile he recommended two bird guide books which he had in stock. Each contained a one-paragraph summary of the hummingbird family (*Trochilidae*), a few cogent facts and color illustrations of the 15 species in the United States. (We later found out that there are 319 species, most of them in Central and South America.)

Armed with these two bird guides, I began trying to match our hummingbirds with those in the books, according to voice, habitat, and "field marks"—or colors. Our first "little redbird," I decided, was probably a male Anna's (*Calypte anna*), described as the only U.S. hummer with both a red crown and throat (gorget) and the only one commonly found in California in midwinter; though it could have been a Costa's (*Calypte costae*), the species with a purple or amethyst throat and crown also common in our area.

"I don't care what the bird books say." Russell shrugged. "I've definitely seen the purples turn red in certain lights."

This phenomenon, which is called iridescence, is a trademark of hummingbirds. There are many beautiful colors in the bird world, including those of the handsome orange and black orioles, red-breasted finches, and yellow wild canaries that continued to freeload from our hummingbird feeders. But there is no mistaking their colors; they are always there and always the same. A hummingbird's colors are unpredictable. They change in a wink from gray to green, from tawny to tangerine, from metallic bronze and gold to glittering purple and red.

Even the brilliant crowns and gorgets (throat feathers) that adorn most male hummers look black when the light fails to capture their iridescence. A photograph needs light from exactly the proper angle to catch any *one* of the bird's colors.

When he learned about the hummingbirds' iridescence, Russell's immediate reaction was relief. "All this time I've been worrying about not catching the colors," he said. "I thought it was because of my eyes."

Even ornithologists, we discovered, have been thoroughly disappointed in attempts to reproduce hummingbird colors. Some have suggested superimposing different metallic inks on conventional colors to produce the iridescent hues.

In my own overzealous wish to be helpful, I matched up two of Russell's prettiest hummingbird pictures with a species I found in my bird guidebooks, the Calliope (*Stellula calliope*). He had caught the same bird in two different positions and its color markings looked exactly the same as those of the Calliope in the bird books, so I named the pictures Calliope I and Calliope II. I felt quite proud of myself as I stuck the gold labels with my husband's name and the bird's name on the back of the pictures. It was the only bird I had dared to identify by species.

A couple of expert hummingbirders came over to see the pictures, raved a while over them, then politely suggested that we not name them according to species.

"*That* is definitely not a Calliope. It's a male Costa's," one informed us. They spent an hour explaining how they had learned to distinguish between these two and other species.

When they left, Russell's comment was "Well, that's like trying to explain how a rose is born. Hummingbirds are like roses. They shouldn't be dissected, they should be enjoyed."

But, I thought, it's time we really learned something about them. I didn't want to make any more mistakes in labeling. And besides, I was beginning to be intrigued by these enchanting little birds.

CHAPTER FIVE

Hummingbirds: Nature's Helicopters

For a whole year Russell did not have to go to the hospital again. And then another year.

He had been in and out of hospitals every year since becoming a diabetic—until the hummingbirds came.

Now he had his up-and-down periods—days when he felt better or worse, when he could see better or not so well—but these were to be expected. What wasn't to be expected was that his general physical condition didn't seem to be getting worse as, with his medical history, it should have been. He was still taking his sixty to eighty units of insulin a day; he still had reactions and other minor complications, but none severe enough to require hospitalizations. It was his longest out-of-hospital intermission in more than thirty years.

His "visual acuity," to use the medical terminology, had

gradually diminished from 10 percent (the point at which one is considered legally blind) to 5, 3, 2, then less than 1 percent. Yet his severe eye hemorrhaging had stopped, and he had not had to go back to Colorado for a laser beam treatment.

The fact was that Russell's physical problems seemed to be in check, and I marveled at the change in him as he became more and more absorbed in the hummingbirds. Call it coincidence, mind over matter, whatever—something was happening within him, and it was more than a rebirth of hope and spirit. He had an inner calm and serenity as he sat or stood for hours on end watching the hummingbirds, working with his seeing-eye equipment—he was constantly redesigning or building new gadgets —and turning out prints in the darkroom.

Most amazing to me was that after all these years, at a time in his life when he had so little left to rejoice over, he seemed actually happier than I had ever known him to be.

The hummingbirds literally had become a "magnificent obsession" with him, and his enthusiasm was contagious. I soon found myself turning from husband-watching to bird-watching. The birds themselves were as fascinating as all the bird-shooting paraphernalia that festooned our front patio.

I started hummingbirding in earnest, with my own feeder hung right outside my study window. Russell was too busy to make me a tonic bottle feeder, so I had to settle for a plastic one. He hung it from the bottom of a redwood planter. The birds were only about three feet away as I worked at my desk.

He Saw a Hummingbird

I made frequent trips to the library and pored over hundreds of musty pages in old or rare books, technical journals, and magazines, only to find that serious hummingbirding, even for the experts, has been a continuous exercise in frustration and has driven ornithologists to the brink of despair trying to figure out the mysteries, contradictions, and idiosyncrasies of these tiny birds.

The more we learned about hummingbirds, and especially how little is known about them, the less concerned we were about our own mistakes.

The hummingbird has presented more problems to science than any other bird. Though the tiniest of avian creatures, it is the biggest bundle of contradictions of any of the bird families. Its habits of courting, mating, nesting, feeding, sleeping, bathing, fighting, *and* flying are peculiarly its own. According to the books it is known especially for its pugnacity and antisocial behavior toward its fellows as well as toward man.

Armed with a few such sketchy facts, my twenty-twenty vision and a pair of binoculars, Russell's seeing eye and supersensory ears, we turned our front patio into a new and truly exciting world of hummingbird-watching. We were rewarded with almost daily delights and never-ending puzzlements.

Walt Whitman once wrote: "You must not know too much or be too precise or scientific about birds and trees and flowers. A certain free margin . . . helps your enjoyment of these things."

Hummingbirds: Nature's Helicopters

These were Russell's sentiments. He honestly didn't care whether a hummingbird was a Calliope or a Costa's or an Anna's or a Rufous.

But I was determined to be as scientifically accurate as possible and made several trips to the library in an effort to learn how to identify the species of birds at our feeders, paying particular attention to the Costa's, Anna's, and Rufous, which I now knew were common in our area. In one comprehensive report on hummingbirds I learned that the Anna's is rose-red but in certain lights turns to purplish red; the Costa's is burnished metallic violet, changing to royal purple, blue, or green in certain lights; the Rufous has a golden gorget, changing to brilliant metallic scarlet in certain lights, and vice versa. No wonder even the experts become confused! One of the most intriguing field marks noted was the white spot behind the eye of the Anna's and Costa's. The Anna's could be identified by a *minute* white spot *immediately* behind the eye, the Costa's by a *small* white spot behind the eye.

Russell's response to this information was a skeptical "Let me know if you see any white spots."

The next morning I took my bird guides and binoculars outside, spread open the books on a patio table, then brought out a pot of coffee and said to Russell, "I've made up my mind. I'm going to stay right here. I'm not going to budge until I identify one of those hummingbirds for certain."

At least a dozen were buzzing all around us, whirling, diving, flashing their fiery colors in the bright morning sunlight, darting and dashing between the feeders and the orange and grapefruit trees.

"Don't forget to look for the white spots," Russell said, as he took his coffee back to the darkroom.

An hour later I was still there, thoroughly engrossed with one little clown that I was about to decide must be definitely an adult male Costa's according to everything I had learned so far. When he was hovering or flying, I couldn't tell: the colors came and went too fast. He would dive straight at me, stop with a jolt, and hover right in front of my nose, but then he was only a tiny dark blur of wing movement. I could see his colors distinctly only when he perched for several minutes at a time on his favorite limb in the grapefruit tree. I stood under the tree and studied him closely. By now I knew it had to be a male because of his brilliant throat and crown, and there was no mistaking the color—it was purple or amethyst.

But it is difficult to identify a species by color alone even after you've caught the colors. The iridescence is only the beginning of the hummingbirder's headaches. One of the distinguishing marks of the Costa's, for example, is that the gorget or throat feathers project greatly at the sides in a sort of distended bib. I went back to my books and looked at the illustrations again. The distended bibs of the Calliope, Lucifer, and Costa's were almost identical—and all purple. But the Lucifer has a curved bill and a deeply forked tail, and is found mostly in Texas, not California. Only the Calliope's throat is purple, not his head. Thus by the process of elimination I decided that I had made my very first for-sure-and-certain identification of a species of hummingbird.

I returned to my spot under the grapefruit tree and stood there scrutinizing the little bird, still perched and preening and glistening in the sun. There was no doubt about it—his head and throat were purple and his throat feathers projected greatly at the sides. I took a few steps to one side, then the other. He was still purple and I could still see the distended bib. For the first time I knew the thrill that all dedicated bird-watchers must experience when they identify a new species for their bird lists.

I stood there gazing up and gleefully chanting, "Hello, little Costa's, you pretty little purple bird, now I know what you are, ho ho ho, you're a Costa's!"

Then suddenly to my absolute and utter astonishment the little Costa's did something that Costa's simply do not do—he started singing! I was aghast. Something was horribly wrong, and ornithologists, of course, will say that I was. Or that perhaps I was hallucinating. Hummingbirds can't sing. They are not songbirds. Everybody knows that. It's one of the very first things you learn when you begin hummingbirding. It's perfectly obvious to anyone who has ever watched and listened to hummingbirds, and in the maze of mysteries and contradictions it's the one point of general agreement among the experts. The hummingbirds' inability to sing is, in fact, regarded

67

as a serious deficiency in such a beautiful and versatile little creature whose talents outshine those of other birds in so many other ways.

Some South American species apparently do try to sing, but those who have heard them say their vocal performance is puny compared with even the poorest of songbirds'. In my library research I had run across an isolated report of a field trip in Arizona during which one of the birders *thought* he heard a Blue-throated hummingbird singing; but no one else in the party heard it, so he concluded the Blue-throat's notes were too high for most human ears.

Of the North American varieties, the only hummer known to sing at all, though not very well, is our own rose-red Anna's. But the bird in our grapefruit tree was not an Anna's. I checked my books again. The Anna's is definitely rose-red, not purple. He does not have a distended bib. His voice is a *chick;* the Costa's voice is a soft *chik,* according to Roger Tory Peterson, the world's number one birder. The Anna's song, which we have heard many times, is a series of squeaking, grating noises, like a rusty hinge or a squeegee on a wet window. The song of the little Costa's was more like a high, squeaky miniature violin, a softer squeak than that of the Anna's.

I stood rooted to the spot, my eyes fixed on him intently to catch every movement, my ears sharpened to make certain the bird was singing, not just *chik-chiking.* There was no question in my mind—the bird was unmistakably singing. I could see his throat movements as he started and stopped. Moreover, his song was accompanied by a fascinating fluttering of his tail in perfect rhythm. When the song stopped, the tail fluttering stopped.

His first concert lasted perhaps ten minutes—I wasn't clocking him—with intermissions. Then he flew off to the red bottle brush tree in the neighbor's yard next door. In a few minutes he was back in the grapefruit tree, perched and singing again.

This time I went back and called Russell from his workshop for consultation. He could distinguish between bird voices better than I could.

"Would you say that bird is singing or not?" I asked, as he stood with me under the tree listening.

"Of course, he's singing. Why?"

He couldn't see the bird or even a flickering of color in the angle of light that hit the bird.

I gave him a briefing: "I've finally identified one species of hummingbird for certain. It's a Costa's. It can't be anything else. But Costa's don't sing. Only the Anna's sing."

"So what's the problem? That one up there is definitely singing."

"That one up there is my Costa's. But according to the books it has to be an Anna's. Can you tell by its voice what it is?"

He listened carefully for a few minutes, then said, "It's definitely not an Anna's . . . nor a Costa's. I'd say he's a Rufous."

69

He Saw a Hummingbird

"He can't be a Rufous. He's the wrong color. And besides, it's not time for the Rufouses yet."

"How do you know? You can't go by everything the books say," he reminded me. "I'll bet there's a lot of cross-breeding among hummingbirds that the experts don't know about yet. Maybe our hummingbirds here are different. . . .

"Maybe the ornithologists should come to Palm Springs to study hummingbirds," he added. Then, teasingly, "Incidentally, have you found any white spots behind the eyes yet?"

I had given up on that project about ten minutes after I started it (and I still have never seen any of the white spots), but I was indeed exuberant over the results of my first session of really concentrated hummingbird-watching. I had not only identified a species but maybe even discovered a new one for the bird listers—a *singing* Costa's!

In my enthusiastic pursuit of hummingbird knowledge I telephoned the bird curator of a well-known American zoo one day and asked if we could come over and visit his special hummingbird aviary, which is widely known to be one of the finest in America, and perhaps photograph some of the birds. I was surprised when he seemed somewhat less than cordial in his response. Reluctantly he explained that it probably wouldn't be worth our time and trouble to make the trip. Their hummingbirds are usually imported from South America; they are difficult to keep or breed in captivity; unfortunately the last shipment was stricken with a strange illness; their current supply of hummingbirds, he said, was "sadly depleted"—down to about three species.

We had more than that in our front yard.

"I wouldn't want to photograph them in captivity anyway, even if I never catch the colors," Russell said. "Hummingbirds don't belong in zoos." A great many zoo keepers, I learned upon checking, feel the same way.

European zoos for years have tried, without notable success, to keep and breed hummingbirds, whose native habitats are confined to the Western Hemisphere. The birds have consistently shunned habitats anywhere else.

After about two years of study we have learned to identify with a fair degree of accuracy (more or less) the six different species that inhabit our private patio-aviary at different times of the year. They are the Costa's and Calliope (almost identical), Anna's and Black-chin (similar to Costa's and Broad-tail), Rufous and Allen's (practically indistinguishable from one another). Sometimes we get a casual visitor from the Rocky Mountains, the Broad-tail (I think). Considering that this adds up to about half of the species in the United States (some experts list thirteen, others fifteen), it provides us with a fairly good variety of birds—and in great numbers—for our personal observations.

Most hummingbird experts, we have discovered, prefer to do their field studies in more exotic places such as the Costa Rican tropics or the rain forests of Brazil, which is understandable because that's where the more exotic birds are, and the most species (over three hundred). It's also where most humming-bird photography is done. However, we consider ourselves lucky that Russell is able to negotiate around our little Palm Springs pad and that so many hummingbirds—dozens at a time —are willing to land here and obligingly shoot their own pictures.

In our personal observations and researching we have tried to take into account the variations and contradictions among the hummingbirds and the birders. But we can speak only for the hummingbirds at our house. We don't know whether their idiosyncrasies apply to species elsewhere.

For that matter, there are probably deviations from most of the supposedly established truths in the bird and animal king-doms. We ran up against one on the day we decided to give our hummingbirds a bath. All hummingbirds, the experts agree, bathe frequently. They will take advantage of water wherever it is found and, if given a vessel with water only half an inch deep, will sometimes sit in it and splash like songbirds. That was something we were anxious to see.

"I'll bet they don't," Russell said. "Remember our raccoons?"

Indeed I did. How could I forget? The raccoons used to visit us each night when we lived at the water's edge of Lake Mar-grethe in northern Michigan. They would raid our garbage barrels and have a feast. One of the known facts of the animal world is that raccoons *always* wash their food before they eat it. Not usually, but *always*. Well, our raccoons didn't. With the lake right there in front of them, they would not wash their food. So we began to set out plates of food for them with a big pan of water right beside it. They couldn't have asked for better service than that. Still they refused to wash their food.

We spent months watching a mother raccoon and her brood during evenings at feeding time and often far into the night foraging around. We were doing a picture story and got dozens of shots in various poses (many were "self-portraits," like the hummingbirds, but with a far simpler shutter-clicking system) —scrambling up a tree or in and out of the garbage barrel or eating off the plates. But not once did we ever seen them washing their food.

However, in the hope of seeing our hummingbirds splash like songbirds in a birdbath, I filled one of my best Italian red pottery soup bowls with water and placed it on a stand between my window feeder and the orange tree, where I could keep a constant watch on it from my study. I left it there for two weeks, filling it with fresh water daily. The bowl was the right color—red. Our hummingbirds will land on or dive at almost anything that is red, including the knobs on some of Russell's tripods. They zipped over and around the red bowl but never in it. They are also supposed to enjoy bathing in the soft spray of a garden hose. We tried this and they didn't like it, either. It may be true that they will take advantage of water wherever it is found—in tropical rain forests. But in the dry desert climate of Palm Springs they don't seem interested in even getting their feet wet, much less splashing like songbirds.

In our two weeks of observing dozens of hummingbirds who are supposed to bathe frequently, we saw not a single one that so much as poked a bill at the birdbath we set out for them. They should have done so out of curiosity, as this is another trait they're well known for, and we've seen their curiosity demonstrated thousands of times in other ways: inspecting cameras, lights, tripods, people's headgear and eyeglasses.

Why did they snub the birdbath? Who knows?

As Russell says, "Why do the swallows come back to Capistrano on the same day each spring?"

Why do hummingbirds who, according to the laws of aerodynamics, shouldn't be able to fly, keep on flying with such audacity?

Russell's answer to that one is, "Nobody told them they can't fly, so they do."

And it may be as good an answer as any to the mystery of my singing Costa's. Someone forgot to tell him he couldn't sing, so he was singing.

From our research and personal observations it didn't take long for us to arrive at a Murphy's law for hummingbirds: the only generalization that can be safely made about hummingbirds is that they can always be counted on to do the unpredictable. With hummingbirds it is best to avoid using the words *always* and *never*. The only exception to this rule is that they will *always* prove you wrong.

HUMMINGBIRDS DON'T PERCH?

Our hummingbirds have disproved beyond any doubt one of the most common assumptions in the bird world.

As amateurs in a highly specialized and complicated branch of ornithology, we would dare to make very few flat statements about hummingbirds with assurance and certainty, but this is one of them. Hummingbirds *do* perch, and quite often, and for long periods at a time. Moreover, from our observations (over a period of more than three years) we found perching to be a predictable, common occurrence and definitely *not* an unpredictable exception to the rule as my singing Costa's (or Russell's Rufous) undoubtedly was.

It was the singing Costa's, in fact, that started me pondering the nonperching myth. I had spent about three hours watching him flying between my feeder, the grapefruit tree, and the bottle brush tree next door, but at the time I was concerned only with his singing, not with his perching. Later I realized he had spent more of his time perching than flying.

Russell and I were not even aware that hummingbirds are

technically classified as "nonpasserine," or nonperching, birds. From the time they started coming to our house they would perch anywhere perching facilities were available, which was just about everywhere—in the citrus trees, on the oleander and pyracantha bushes, on our hanging planters and feeders.

We simply took for granted that hummingbirds perched, since we watched them doing it every day, until people started telling us they didn't. This began with Russell's first perching pictures. Everyone who saw them invariably remarked in a tone of skepticism, "But I've never seen a hummingbird perched." Or, "I didn't know hummingbirds perched." Or, more often and more emphatically, "But hummingbirds don't perch." As if it were a photographic gimmick.

Actually it was a gimmick in a way, but not in the way they thought. A perched hummingbird is not nearly as photogenic as one hovering or in flight with outspread tail or wings (which is undoubtedly why bird books rarely contain photographs of hummingbirds perched), but Russell wanted some perching shots for variety. It would have been impossible for him to move his seeing-eye camera around and catch the birds perched in a tree or bush; and it would have been unthinkable for him to do it the easy way and merely replace his bottle feeder for a while on the lampstand by a commercial plastic feeder with perches. Instead he made his own perch and attached it to the lampstand just below the feeder spout and the hummingbirds of course came and perched.

Hummingbirds: Nature's Helicopters

One of the widely circulated nonperching myths is that hummingbirds always hover while feeding. Give a hummingbird a perch and he'll use it instead of hovering at the feeder. Why should he expend energy the equivalent of about ten times that of a man running nine miles an hour when he can sit there and sip without exerting himself?

And why should he expend energy hovering from flower to flower when he can get his artificial nectar at the feeder?

As Russell says, "Hummingbirds aren't stupid. They could teach humans a lot about energy conservation."

One day I clocked a little Costa's who was perched on a pyracantha twig just outside my window—within arm's reach if the window were open, and about ten inches from my feeder. He sat there for exactly forty-five minutes without bestirring himself except for one quick sip (five seconds) at the feeder, thus also disproving another commonly accepted belief: that hummingbirds must feed every ten or fifteen minutes. They *usually* do. But not *always*.

Hummingbirds are supposed to have very weak feet and legs. This is often cited as the reason they can't walk or hop around on the ground like other birds and why they spend most of their time flying, seldom perching. Yet I have watched many a hummer clamp his tiny feet around the perch on my feeder and hang in there forking his tongue in the sugar water—with a big finch four times his size hogging the opposite side of the perch and rocking the feeder to a ninety-degree angle. I have sat there mesmerized, thinking for sure the hummingbird is going to fall off backwards, but he never does. He usually outlasts the finch at the feeder perch.

Those who acknowledge that hummingbirds sometimes do perch will tell you they always choose the highest branches of a tree, never a low branch, and never among dense foliage. Our birds may have a peculiar streak of perversity in them, but two of their favorite perching spots are the lowest branch on our orange tree overlooking the nasturtium bed and the twisted bramble of dead twigs on the pyracantha bush at my window. We should have trimmed those twigs off long ago, but we have left them because the hummingbirds like to perch there between feedings. And I have often spotted them in the dense foliage of our citrus trees and oleanders, sitting there. Perched. For long periods of time. I'll admit it requires good eyesight to spot them and they're only little dark blobs, not the charming, bejeweled, spectacular winged creatures you see in flight or hovering. But they *are* hummingbirds and they *are* perching.

According to scientific studies, they do perch at night while sleeping. We have never seen them sleeping. At nighttime, after feeding, they fly off over the oleanders. They are back at dawn the next morning.

Perhaps the reason their daytime perching habits have been overlooked by bird-watchers is that their marvels of flight and hovering are far more bewitching to watch. We certainly would go along with that.

But there are also certain marvels to behold in a hummingbird perched if the eyes of the beholder are looking in the right place. As for instance in a grapefruit tree where a sunbeamed purple Costa's, perching and preening, flutters his tail and starts singing.

At the very moment I wrote these words, I heard the familiar loud buzzing whir that I recognized, without looking, as that of a Rufous or Allen's. I stopped typing and turned to watch the bird standing perched, tiny feet clamped around the edge of the feeder *lid*—I had long since deliberately removed the perches —and drinking with his bill downward instead of the more normal upward position of hovering.

I was astonished. The slippery plastic feeder lid must be a difficult thing for the little bird to hang onto. Obviously he preferred that to hovering without a perch at the lower side feeder holes as a tiny mauve baby bird was doing at that moment.

The beauty of the bird perched on the lid was breathtaking. Its black-tipped, bright orange tail was spread out like a minia-ture fan. Its green and gold back glistened in the sunlight. I knew instantly that it was either a female Rufous or a male Allen's. Their coloring is almost identical. With a free margin for error I mentally listed it as a Rufous, which to my mind is the most beautiful of all our hummingbirds, the most colorful and the most fiery-tempered. Only a Rufous would cling so tenaciously to such a precarious perch as a plastic lid.

79

He Saw a Hummingbird

From my close-range observation post I have also been bewitched on innumerable occasions by a pair of hummingbirds beginning their courtship ritual with one bird perched on a pyracantha twig and the other hovering above.

Anyone who has not seen these exquisite little nonpasserine birds perching has missed one of the true wonders of the hummingbird world.

FEEDING

The hummingbird's diet consists mainly of sugar (nectar) for its high energy needs, and protein, which it gets from insects. We have observed that our hummingbirds feed on sugar water, flowers, and insects in that order. Curiously they seem to much prefer the artificial nectar in our feeders to the real thing in our flowers.

This is in spite of the fact that we have a great variety of "hummingbird flowers" known to be their favorites. Hummingbirds, in fact, are so closely associated with flowers that in Brazilian Portuguese they are known as the *beija-flor*, or "flower kisser."

Although we have never actually clocked their feeding time, our off-the-cuff calculations would add up to about 90 percent at the sugar-water bottles as against 10 percent at the flowers. Our feeders are never empty. We make sure of that. When it comes time to refill one, if there is a hummer feeding, as there usually is, he expresses his annoyance in no uncertain squeaks and twitterings as we take his bottle away. Then he flies to a twig and perches until we bring it back filled, never discommoding himself to dine cafeteria style at the blossoming flower beds and shrubbery. He prefers room service in his sybaritic avian life-style.

We have decided that hummingbirds, like some people, are opportunists, with a canny talent for freeloading wherever food is available, getting the most with the least effort.

Apparently, however, they have remarkable stamina in searching for food when necessary, reportedly following their food flowers in vertical and horizontal directions over great changes in altitude and distance, moving up and down mountains and across deserts. Though the smallest of the bird kingdom, they are also known as the hardiest (authorities estimate their life-span at eight to twelve years), thriving from low desert habitats to the peaks of Ecuador.

According to experts who have studied the migratory habits of hummingbirds, they are not long-distance migrants. They may be wandering gypsies in their search for food, but they do not usually wander too far from their native habitats. The exceptions are the Rufous, Ruby-throat, and Calliope. Of these the Rufous holds the record, traveling some two thousand miles by an overland route from Alaska to its winter home in Mexico, a prodigious journey for a birdling weighing only three or four grams. But the Ruby-throat's nonstop flight of more than five hundred miles across the Gulf of Mexico to Yucatán is usually cited as evidence of the astonishing toughness and tenacity of these tiniest of avian bodies.

What the Ruby-throat does for food during this journey remains a mystery.

And where the Rufouses go when they leave our house we wouldn't venture to guess, but we would place bets on their knowing every ten- or fifteen-minute feeder and flower stop between Alaska and Mexico.

A common belief is that hummingbirds, because of their minute size and high energy requirements, *must* feed every ten or fifteen minutes in order to survive. This may be their normal routine. Some of ours seem to be hungry all the time. But the Costa's I clocked feeding only once in forty-five minutes survived his fast very well. And several hummingbirds have survived long periods without food—in our own house. They would fly in accidentally and become trapped there, in a panic, not knowing how to get out the same door they came in. Fortunately we have never had any fatalities. Once a hummingbird flew in at nine o'clock in the morning, zoomed back and forth under our high-beamed ceiling, finally landed on one of the beams, and perched there for hours. About three o'clock in the afternoon (six hours without food) he began trying again to get out, hit the sharp edge of a picture frame, and fell to the floor. When I picked him up, I saw the bleeding wound on his head. He appeared to be lifeless. But I hurriedly took him out to the feeder and pointed his bill into it, and he drank and took off as though nothing had happened to him.

Initially we didn't know what to do with a hummingbird trapped in the house. But we soon learned. One flew into Russell's workshop one day and we lured him out by hanging a bottle of sugar water in front of the door.

We also learned that it was best not to try to catch the bird or to shoo him toward an exit, which would only panic him more, but to let him fly around or perch as long as he wanted until he found an open door or window. We immediately remove the window screens and open the windows when a bird flies in the house, and usually it soon finds its way out.

From our observations we feel certain that a hummingbird's survival depends a great deal on his unique ability to conserve energy at every opportunity—by perching as often or as long as he needs to between feedings.

We have also found that our hummingbirds get most of their proteins while perching. I have watched *my* little birds on the pyracantha twigs sit there day after day snapping up insects with their darting tongues, which look like long silver threads. We have also watched the hummers perched in the oleanders where the bug-catching is easy. They are quite adept at snatching their proteins in flight when they need to, as we have observed from the vantage point of Russell's feeder. In fact, their proficiency at this has led us to conclude that a hummingbird's eyes must be among the most amazing of their physical endowments.

We can offer only conjecture, but we believe that humming-birds can see through the back of their heads. We have often seen them dart *backwards* to catch an insect several yards *behind* them that they could not possibly have seen from their front-ward position at the feeder.

Russell, of course, cannot see all the bug-snatching that I see. One day I found a couple of overripe pears impaled on a long stick near his seeing eye.

"And what is *this* for?"

"You said they need their protein."

He had bought the softest, most overripe pears he could find at the supermarket especially for the hummingbirds. "They'll draw plenty of bugs," he said blithely. If there was one more thing I didn't need on the front lawn it was rotten pears. I assured him the little dears would do fine without them.

NESTING

Most people enjoy finding a bird's nest of any kind and watching the mother and baby birds. We were eager to find a hummingbird's nest with birds to photograph. Hummingbirds are known to be geniuses at hiding their nests where no one can find them, and we have never found one at our house. But we have seen a few at other homes and, with typical perverse audacity, the birds had built them in the most conspicuous places, right under the noses of people traffic. One was on top of a set of oriental wind chimes hanging directly above the front door. When we were there a party was going on inside and people wandered in and out to look at the mother bird on her nest with two tiny white eggs in it.

Another nest was built in a hanging artificial flower pot on the front porch of a mobile home, again only a few feet outside the front door. There were two baby birds it in. The nest was hanging at eye level and we watched in horror as the mother hummingbird kept jabbing her long beak down the baby birds' throats, feeding them. Why baby hummingbirds aren't stabbed to death during feeding is another of their well-kept mysteries. Hummingbirds have long, needlelike bills enclosing the thread-like tongue, which is forked and tubular; its split halves fit together into a drinking straw.

We were told about a perfect location for photographing two newborn hummingbirds. They were in a nest built in a pool-side bush in the corner of an enclosed patio—in full view of everyone. The only problem was that when we arrived and looked in the nest, the baby birds appeared to be quite dead.

Their tiny beaks were turned straight up, their eyes were

closed, they didn't move. The mother bird was nowhere around, or at least not in sight. We decided she had abandoned her babies. We left, depressed that we had seen baby hummingbirds dead.

A couple of days later we received a call from the lady of the house telling us the birds were alive. She had thought they were dead, too. We went back with camera, lights, and tripod, and, with a little help from me in focusing, Russell got his first pictures of a mother and baby hummers in the nest—which he couldn't see until the pictures were enlarged and printed.

Later we found out why the baby birds had appeared to be lifeless. Hummingbirds are able to go into a state of suspended animation like lizards. Their beaks go straight up, their metabolism is lowered, and heartbeat and breathing slow. Often they appear to be quite dead. The baby birds we thought were dead were merely sleeping.

Hummingbirds do not sleep like other birds, with head tucked under a wing or laid back. Instead, they become torpid to conserve energy.

We learned that their awakening from their state of torpidity had a deep religious significance. Early missionaries to South America used the "awakening of the hummingbirds" to make the Indians understand the miracle of the resurrection. Thus the hummingbird became a symbol of everlasting life.

How strange that Russell's awakening from the dark tunnel

of blindness should begin with a hummingbird, itself the symbol of the greatest of all miracles.

CAT PATROL

Popular myth to the contrary, the fact is that a cat *can* catch a hummingbird. I learned this the hard way.

I had no sooner settled into my serious birding with feeder and guidebooks than I saw Sylvester skulking across the front yard. He was the big gray-and-black-striped wild cat known as the neighborhood menace.

"Maybe the mockingbirds will take care of him," we said hopefully. Mockingbirds can be holy terrors, attacking dogs, cats, and humans with equal ferocity, as we had learned from personal experience. We had seen the mockingbirds swoop down on our poodle, Gogi, and the friendly Siamese cat who often wandered in and out of our house from her home beyond our backyard fence of oleanders. We had never had a cat problem until Sylvester came. The mockingbirds did not scare him away. Neither could we. Our property was completely fenced in, but he found ways of crawling under or over.

87

He Saw a Hummingbird

"He can't catch the hummingbirds," Russell said. "They're too quick for him."

Nevertheless I didn't like the way he came slinking toward my feeder and sat crouching there, half hidden under the pyracantha bush. I began a regular routine of early-morning cat patrol duty. By 5:30 A.M. I was usually outside, with a cup of coffee, newspapers, and bird books spread on the patio table —and a garden hose clamped in my left hand, ready to spray at the push of a button.

The "water repellent," or light spray from a hose, is not harmful and works with most cats. Not with Sylvester. I finally called the man of the house where Sylvester lived—when he was home. I introduced myself and explained as tactfully as possible the problem with his cat and our hummingbirds. It turned into a fascinating phone conversation.

"Lady, it's not my cat. It's my son's. I don't even like cats," he said. "And my wife has asthma, so we can't have a cat in the house. If I had my way I'd take him out and dump him. Why don't you buy a BB gun and start shooting him? You can't hurt him, you'll just sting him. It's against the law to shoot a BB gun within the city limits," he explained, "but I'm not going to tell on you and I'm sure the neighbors won't. They've all tried to get rid of that cat."

"Maybe your son could keep the cat on a leash, or put a bell around his neck," I suggested.

"That would spook him out. Cats are free spirits. They're supposed to roam. That's nature," he said.

So Sylvester remained a free spirit roaming among our hummingbirds until one morning I saw it happen as I was scooping the bird books from my desk to go out and take up my post as cat sentry.

There was a sudden thunderous thrashing in the pyracantha bush beneath my window and I looked out just in time to see the gleaming streak of a purple Costa's disappear into the cat's mouth.

I was horrified.

But one's personal grief at the loss of a hummingbird—or any other bird or animal—is relatively insignificant in the overall perspective of nature. Who are we, after all, to intercede in the conflict between cat and birds, trying to rearrange nature?

We think, however, there is a lesson to be learned from our experience that other hummingbird lovers may appreciate and benefit by: for all their renowned swiftness and maneuverability, hummingbirds are *not*, as commonly supposed, immune from danger at ground level. They spend a great deal of time *very close* to the ground, a fact that I have never found mentioned in my researches, and one that from our personal observations would seem to be worth a warning. It is generally assumed that hummingbirds, the aerial acrobats of the bird world, are too quick to be caught by anything. Not true. They have reportedly been captured by snakes, frogs, praying mantises, and dragonflies. But their mortality rate is low compared with that of most birds. The major hazards of a hummingbird's life are window panes and spiders' webs.

In the enchantment of watching their high-flying antics, it is easy to miss the shimmering action nearer the ground. We have often seen our hummingbirds spinning like tops or feathered corkscrews downward to within inches of the earth, and on other occasions hovering motionless for minutes at a time over the nasturtium bed under our orange tree—tiny tails spread out like miniature fans, wings beating so fast they look like the translucent four wings of a dragonfly, crowns and gorgets sparkling in the sunlight. . . . They are spellbinding to watch at any level, whether ricocheting like bullets over our red-tiled roof or hurtling at the usual hummingbird velocity toward the big red blossoming bottle brush tree next door. But as they hang shimmying among our nasturtium blossoms, almost at ground level, their awesome beauty leaves me sometimes holding my breath with fear.

The dog and cat problem is a difficult one for all bird lovers to face. Both dogs and cats have the predatory instinct. Yet it is possible for all of them to live in harmony. We know one hummingbirding couple with four big hummingbird feeders, swarms of birds, and four big cats. The cats are well-trained house pets who are in and out of the house all day long, underneath the dozens of hummers whirring among feeders and foliage. The cats were trained, with the light spray of a garden hose, not to bother the birds.

As for Sylvester, I went to the "animal control" place one day to pick up a cat trap, recommended by everyone as our solution to the bird and cat problem, and came home instead with a dog. I didn't know that "animal control" was the city dog pound until I got there. The lady pound-keeper said, "What you need is a dog." She disappeared briefly behind a swinging wooden door, engulfed in a sad cacophany of barking dogs, and returned with a little white furry thing in her arms.

There was an instant bond between us. I signed the adoption papers on the spot and walked out with the pup, a female mix of poodle and terrier named Calliope, a name I chose hastily when the lady pound-keeper, noting a blank space on the adoption papers, said, "We need a name here."

"Okay. Calliope." It was the only name I could think of at the moment. "It's a hummingbird," I explained, spelling the name out for her. She gave me a peculiar look.

I took Calliope to a vet down the street for her shots and checkup. He pronounced her in good health and about nine months old. I stopped at a pet shop and bought puppy food, rubber balls and bones, a collar and leash. I took her home and put her in Russell's arms and said, "Surprise! Here's your anniversary present."

He wasn't exactly thrilled.

I showed him the dog's tail, a long, spiraling appendage of questionable origin that waved like a semaphore and should be relatively easy for him to see. And what would happen to her if we left her in the pound? Of course he melted.

Calliope took care of our cat problem. She became my second helper on cat patrol duty. We never saw Sylvester again.

HUMMINGBIRDS ANTISOCIAL?

Once you get into hummingbirding it is surprising how many people come up with their own special hummingbird stories. One of the best recorded by ornithologists is that of an artist who lay sick for a year in a California sanatorium with a feeder hung outside his bedroom window. A little fiery-tempered Rufous took over, chasing away all intruders. His presence and antics cheered the invalid and hastened his recovery, and when he was finally permitted to go outside in a wheelchair, the Rufous followed, hovering in front of the man's eyes. When the convalescing artist returned home in a car, the Rufous somehow followed him to his house, eight miles away. To regain his strength, the artist began daily walks and was always accompanied by the hummingbird flying along with him or ahead of him and perching until his human companion caught up.

After he was fully recovered, the artist went back to work in the city, and a month had passed before he returned to his home in the mountains for a weekend visit. He was barely out of his car when the little Rufous appeared, whizzing around his head and dancing back and forth before his eyes. The Rufous was not fed on his walks with the artist, though he probably visited flowers and caught insects along the way. He apparently was attached to the man because he liked his company.

I'm sure this was why Russell developed such a quick rapport with the hummingbirds.

When he first started working with them, I was often away from home on assignments, and he spent hours alone with them on the front patio, listening to them and talking to them individually.

As he once explained it, "When you're by yourself a lot, you get lonesome. Well, I was lonesome and I had no one else to talk to, so I started talking to the hummingbirds."

I'm sure this was why our first Little Redbird kept coming back. It was for something more than just his sugar water. Like the little Rufous with his artist friend, Little Redbird became attached to Russell apparently because he liked his company.

In our minds there is no doubt that hummingbirds do respond to the friendship of a man or woman who cares about them in other ways besides merely providing food for them, though some experts maintain that this is the exception rather than the rule and that they are antisocial toward humans as well as toward each other. Some claim they are totally devoid of affection, sometimes even hostile to the point of actually attacking people. We simply don't believe this.

However, it is easy to understand how such rumors start. I still often duck my head or throw up my arms for protection when I see them coming. We have seen and heard them whiz up to within an inch of our heads innumerable times as though about to attack. Then incredibly they make an abrupt turn and miss us or just as frequently jolt to a dead stop directly in front of us and hang there hovering in midair, curiously looking us over, eyeball to eyeball. It's probably their idea of fun.

They are astonishingly tame, but only up to a certain point. They can be approached closer than other birds, yet they do not allow themselves to become house pets easily. As usual, there are exceptions to the rule. One of the most remarkable exceptions we ever heard of was the story of Pretty Bird, a baby hummer that had fallen from its nest and was found by a friend of ours, Marion Shea, and her teenage daughter, Selene, while they were walking their dog. They took the bird home, put it in a shoe box, and nourished it back to health with sugar water fed from an eyedropper. When he was well and strong enough to set free, they took him outside and let him go. To their amazement he was back chic-chicing at their door a few minutes later. He became so tame he would come when they called him by name. He grew dependent on the eyedropper feedings. The Sheas would let him out of the house about six o'clock each morning and he would perch most of the day on a hibiscus bush by their kitchen window—waiting for them to come out and feed him at intervals with his eyedropper.

Later he became more independent and would disappear for several hours at a time, but he always came back at night to sleep in the house in his shoe box and to be fed from the eyedropper.

Pretty Bird spent about a year with the Sheas, flying in and out of the house in total freedom. One day he flew away and didn't come back. Marion thinks he was seduced by a girl friend and lived happily ever after. No one can convince her that hummingbirds are antisocial or devoid of affection. "I think they can be as sensitive and affectionate toward people as people are toward them," she says, "but they need to know that they are free to come and go."

PUGNACITY

One point of general agreement among hummingbird experts is that hummingbirds are the most pugnacious, the most fiery-tempered, and the least family-oriented of all birds. Male hummingbirds are known as fickle fathers, deserting the nest and leaving the care and feeding of baby birds entirely to the mother hummer.

The general picture is that hummingbirds spend most of their time squabbling and fighting, fussin' and feudin' at the feeder, bickering and battling—so antisocial and hostile toward each other that they never fly in flocks or pairs as other birds do, preferring to do their own thing alone rather than in company with others.

For some reason we cannot explain, the hummingbirds at our house do not fit this picture. I don't know how many birds it takes to make a flock, but I have often counted as many as a dozen in a single sighting, which is quite a lot considering the speed with which they move. During early morning and evening rush hours at the feeders, when the activity is greatest, we can't begin to count them. Russell sees only movements and sometimes colors. The actual bird count is up to me. As I have mentioned, one should never use the words *never* or *always* with hummingbirds. But I cannot recall ever seeing a hummingbird around our house without at least three or four others nearby, and usually more than that.

I would even go so far as to say that our hummingbirds are *always* in pairs, threesomes, foursomes, or bunches, *never* in singles. Compared with our other birds, they have a super-abundance of family togetherness. We have a plentiful supply of finches, wild canaries, orioles, and mockingbirds. Except for the finches, which seem to be everywhere all the time, most of them are far more "loners" than our hummingbirds. I have never seen more than one wild canary at a time perched in the pyracantha twigs (and it's one of their favorite spots), or more than two orioles at a time in our orange tree (their favorite), or more than three or four mockingbirds at one time on our roof or the telephone wires.

We see many more hummingbirds at any hour of the day. If they are not family-oriented, it seems curious to us that they would want to hang around together.

We usually cannot distinguish between the sexes of hummingbirds in flight, but ours do their flying, fighting, feeder-squabbling, and hovering in pairs, not singly, and most frequently with a few others getting into the act. They are the Sinatras of the bird world. In vocal performance, life-style, and behavioral patterns they could scarcely be called little choir angels. They do things *their* way.

And nowhere is this more superbly demonstrated than in the billing-and-cooing department.

If hummingbirds do their courting only in certain seasons, as the books say, then our hummingbirds either ignore the seasons, which presumably would be biologically unnatural, or they are possessed of an ardor and affection for one another that has escaped chroniclers of hummingbird lovemaking.

As I sit here at my typewriter day after day, almost within

arm's reach of the hummingbirds, and watching them through a screened window, I have seen their slender, graceful little bodies hang suspended in midair in a perpendicular, bill-to-bill hovering position of incredible beauty. They are not hovering side by side but straight up and down; the bird below stands on its tail with long bill pointed upward; the bird above is hovering *upside down* with its bill touching the upturned one.

They look like the two sections of a Chinese sand timer, or what is more commonly known as a three-minute egg timer, but joined together with their long needle bills and with the wingbeat so fast it is barely visible.

Thus suspended and linked two-in-one with only the tips of their bills touching, they move up and down in perfect perpendicular balance, as though on a magnetic axis; still bill-to-bill they swing back and forth like a pendulum, and then, with a sudden switch of gears and disconnecting of bills, their slow-motion hovering turns into high-speed darting and diving. The upside-down bird barrel-rolls himself right side up. Together they make a downward dive toward the ground, then swing up again and fly off side by side.

Sometimes the upside-down hovering occurs while one bird is resting on a twig and another approaches it in flight, comes to an abrupt stop, and hovers above the perched bird, their bills touching. The perched bird either remains perched during the wooing, or darts off the twig and hovers in the air under the upside-down bird in the sand-timer position.

Hummingbirds: Nature's Helicopters

Almost every day since I began watching our hummingbirds closely, I have seen these displays of affection right outside my window. As I write this, a female hummer hovers at my feeder, then perches on a pyracantha twig; a male comes and hovers above with his beak pointed downward and hers upturned; they confer in soft castanet love talk and move gracefully into an up-and-down pendulum dance, then twirl away toward the grapefruit tree still in their rhythmic vertical yo-yo bounces. An instant later they zip off in a horizontal streak, merrily chasing each other.

It is true they can become fearsomely pugnacious in defending their feeders, which sometimes leads to rather ferocious fighting, but this is also true of other birds, especially our finches. The difference is that the hummingbirds do their battling more beautifully because they are more agile. They are fearless and bold with other birds as well. We have often seen them dive-bomb the finches and orioles away from feeders or trees. From my window I have watched a hummingbird take after a wild canary, driving it away from the feeder, in and out of the orange tree, and finally over the oleanders and out of the yard.

Most of the hummingbirds' wild chases and battles, we think, are done more in sport than in hostility. They seem to enjoy fighting for the fun of it.

The whys and wherefores of hummingbird behavior are exceedingly complex even for experts. Why our hummingbirds should be any more sociable and family-oriented than those elsewhere we don't know. It is conceivable that hummingbirds behave differently according to location and environmental conditions. Most scientific studies of hummingbirds have been made under more controlled conditions than ours, usually of birds in captivity in enclosed aviaries and glass cages, and usually in South America because that's where most of the birds are. It's possible the tropical breeds are more belligerent than ours or that they don't like being caged up for observation.

It's possible they do not have adequate perching facilities or air space around them or the proper atmosphere for fun and romance. Our experience is limited. We have never set eyes on a hummingbird aviary except our own open-air patio, but even here I have noticed the difference in hummingbird behavior between the birds at my window feeder and Russell's, which is in the center of the patio lawn, in direct sunlight for his photographic purposes, and with no perching places available to the birds except when he wants a perching picture and then attaches a perch to the lampstand.

Thus ordinarily the birds at his feeder are there strictly for food and are usually seen hovering and feeding, not playing, jousting, frolicking, courting, dancing, perching, and romancing as they do among the twigs of the pyracantha bush beside my feeder and the blossoms in the hanging redwood planter above my feeder. Also, my feeder is in a shadier spot,

100

partially protected by our tile eaves and of course by the green pyracantha branches—though the hummers prefer the dead jutting twigs as perches because they are closer to the feeder.

It would seem reasonable to assume that the environmental conditions around my feeder are more conducive to normal hummingbird behavior and sociability than those around Russell's. In any case, we have never seen the kind of activity at his feeder that takes place at mine.

This difference right in our own front yard suggests that hummingbird behavior does depend to some extent on where the birds happen to be and what conditions prevail. A great deal of hummingbird research in recent years has been done in Brazil at the world's largest hummingbird aviary, a flying enclosure 160 feet long, 50 feet wide, and 20 feet high, and usually housing some four hundred birds. This is not quite as large as our 175-by-75-foot property with open sky miles high. If we had four hundred hummingbirds hemmed in under a roof 20 feet high, we can't imagine what they might do to each other.

Certainly the behavior of the hummingbirds coming to our house over a period of three years does not square at all with their antisocial reputation. It may be because they're only doing what comes naturally in Palm Springs.

POETRY OF FLIGHT

We had been watching our hummingbirds for quite a while when a friend of ours, a pilot who flies his own plane, casually remarked as he admired Russell's pictures, "You know hummingbirds can't fly. That is, they're not supposed to. They're not built to fly. Their wing and body structure makes it anatomically impossible for them to fly according to the laws of aerodynamics."

This was news to us. But it is indeed true, as we learned when we began checking it out with the experts. Hummingbirds are not structurally built to fly according to human laws of aerodynamics. Yet one point of universal agreement among experts and nonexperts is that hummingbirds *can* fly and they can do things in flight that no other bird can do.

We have seen a hummingbird in full flight stop dead with such a jolt that if it had been an airplane braking instead, the plane would have lost its wings, tail, engine, and all accessories, including the pilot, in the process.

Charles A. Lindbergh once wrote (in an article for *Reader's Digest*) that he came to a crucial decision while on a safari in Africa:

"Lying under an acacia tree," he said, "with the sounds of dawn around me, I realized . . . what man should never overlook: that the construction of an airplane, for instance, is simple when compared with the evolutionary achievement of a bird; that airplanes depend upon advanced civilization; and that where civilization is most advanced, few birds exist.

"I realized that if I had to choose, I would rather have birds than airplanes."

No bird is funnier or more amusing to watch than the hummingbird. I am often startled to find myself in a spontaneous outburst of laughter at the antics I see outside my window; and sometimes, forgetting, I call Russell in to look at them. I keep hoping he can see them, but he sees the movements and colors only at his own feeder. From my perspective all the renowned feats of the world's best circus aerialists and stunt pilots are amateurish compared with the incredible performance of the hummingbirds.

Of all their flight performances the hummers' hovering act is the most fascinating to watch, perhaps because we see more of it, at closer range and for longer periods. Hummingbirds are usually seen hovering at a feeder or a flower bed, but we have seen them as often hovering out there in space, dangling, dancing, or standing on their tails in midair, apparently looking over the territory and deciding where to light next. Although their hovering is usually described as motionless, actually it only appears to be. The hummer's wings are beating about fifty times a second in a vibrating blur, but the body is held quite still in the air. No other bird can fly so competently—and beautifully—in this stationary state of airborne suspension.

We have watched in endless amusement as our finches, determined little mimics, clumsily flutter and shake and shimmy around our feeders, trying incessantly to imitate the hummingbirds' hovering. They usually wind up flitter-flopping to the ground, but they get up and try again. They deserve E for effort.

Hummingbirds are often called "nature's helicopters" because they can go straight up and down, flying vertically or backward and forward as well as sideways. But they are about twice as efficient as the helicopter in fuel consumption per unit of weight. And far more spectacular to watch.

The other day, for instance, I saw a Rufous (or Allen's) shoot straight up from our orange tree and go skimming across the sky in straight up-and-down perpenditcular position like a tiny, shiny golden bullet. It didn't even look like a bird, and I wouldn't have known it was one if I hadn't seen it take off from the tree. I watched it until it disappeared completely from sight. Not once while I watched did it straighten out and fly forward with head and tail in horizontal position as most ordinary birds do.

Another remarkable feat of the hummingbird is flying upside down, although you need a quick eye to catch this. It usually happens if a bird is suddenly assailed from the front: for example, while hovering at a flower or feeder. The surprised hummer turns a backward somersault by flipping its spread tail forward, then goes into a reverse gear on its back with its feet up for a short distance. It then does a barrel roll, turns itself rightside up, and continues whatever flight frolics suit its fancy at the moment. This is one of the regular acts in front of my bird-watching window, and we have occasionally seen it at Russell's feeder.

How can a hummingbird do all these things?

The secret lies in the special design and structure of its flying apparatus, especially the wings and the muscles that move them. But these are technical details best left to the experts in hummingbird anatomy.

The only limitation to the hummingbird's competence in the air is its inability to soar, according to most research. Yet we have often seen our hummingbirds soar on motionless wings from our trees to the red bottle brush next door and back again. True, they do not circle and glide as marvelously as sea gulls. But, from our observations, they *can* soar when they want to or need to, perhaps to conserve energy as they do in perching. And most probably to prove how wrong you can be about hummingbirds.

Meanwhile, as I became more engrossed in watching the hummingbirds and learning about them, Russell continued to make the most of his own limitations and mistakes, occasionally turning out a print that almost halfway pleased him. But many till went into his pile of rejects. We came close to a minor family crisis over one of his rejects. It was a picture of his first Little Redbird and the only one he ever got of the hummingbird he was really trying to catch. But the picture that came out of the darkroom was not at all like the real bird. It was more like a snow bird, an ethereal-looking creature with snow-white head and chest, and dark dim outlines of wings and beak fading into a Chinese-red background.

He wasn't even going to show it to me. I found it on top of his stack of rejects one morning. He snatched it away from me. "I don't want anyone to see *that*."

"Why not?"

"It's terrible."

"I like it. I'm going to have it framed."

"Oh no you're not."

Oh yes I am, I said to myself.

"Photographically it's no good. Anyone can see that," he said. "I'd be ashamed for anyone to see it. The colors are all wrong. You can't even tell it's a hummingbird. I'll get some better pictures of him when I get my bird shooter working better. . . ."

But by the time he had his bird shooter working better, or to his satisfaction, more or less—he never could stop trying to make it work better—the little redbird had stopped coming. I sneaked the picture from the reject pile again and took it in my study and hid it.

He did not reject all his mistakes, however. An accidental

double exposure, with the same bird in different positions, turned out so well that he began trying deliberately for double and triple exposures.

One of these, a triple exposure that looked like three birds, and one that he had worked long and hard to achieve, finally met with his approval sufficiently for him to make a sixteen-by-twenty print of it. Most of his prints were five-by-sevens; only a few were eight-by-tens. The size indicated his approval rate. The triple exposure was the first picture he accepted as good enough for a large print. If *he* thought it was good, then I knew it had to be.

I made up my mind right then that I was going to make a very bold move. I knew he would disapprove, so I didn't tell him. I asked him to go through all his smaller prints and transparencies and pick out two more that *he* thought were good enough for the sixteen-by-twenty enlargements; I would have the three of them framed to hang in our den, now called the Hummingbird Room.

I had a bit of trouble persuading him. He did not think any of his pictures were good enough to waste the large-size paper on. Besides, even small frames were expensive, it would cost too much to have the big ones framed, he was going to start making his own frames for the small ones, he said.

They might not be as fancy as the ones we had had done by a professional framer, but they would be perfectly good enough for his dinette-workshop, he assured me.

107

He Saw a Hummingbird

With my urging and prodding, he finally relented and made two more of the large prints, one of a hummingbird perched and one a front view of a hummer in flight. I took the three of them to the framers. I could hardly wait to pick them up.

CHAPTER SIX

The Exhibit

When the manager of the framing store called to say the pictures were ready, I slipped three more bird prints into a large envelope and went to collect the framed ones.

The manager came up to me as I was paying the bill and said, "You know, we've had a lot of interest among our customers in these pictures. They're beautiful and very unusual. Have you ever thought of having an exhibit of them? I'm sure our gallery downstairs would be interested."

"I'll ask my husband about it," I said.

The suggestion bolstered my confidence in what I had already made up my mind to do. I loaded the big framed pictures into the car and drove over to one of our largest and best art galleries, which I knew only by reputation. I had never been inside it. I went in on the pretense of looking at the current exhibit. A man walked up to me and I asked, "Are you the owner?"

"Yes, can I help you?"

"I collect clown paintings. I see you don't have any."

"Clowns!" He sniffed. "I show only fine art, mostly French Impressionists."

At least it was an opener. I admired the paintings on the walls and then asked casually, "Do you happen to know anything about photography?"

"A little," he said. "I'm interested in photographic art. It's very in, these days."

"I'm looking for an expert to give me an objective appraisal of some pictures I have."

"I'll be happy to. Where are they?"

"In my car. I'll bring them in."

I carried the pictures in one at a time. He set them on a table against the wall, looked at them, and said in a tone of obvious surprise, "This is very good work. Excellent photographic technique and artistically quite stunning—for photography. Most unusual. Who did them?"

"My husband."

"What is he doing with them? Is he a professional bird photographer?"

"No. He was a commercial photographer. Now he's doing this as a hobby, more or less."

"Why isn't he marketing them? They're very commercial, you know. Bird pictures are always in demand. And hummingbirds, my God! Where does he get the hummingbirds?"

"In our front yard."

He gave me a peculiar look and asked, "Does he have any more pictures like these? I assume he must have. . . ."

"He only started this recently," I fibbed. "These are the only big ones we have framed, but I brought a few others I was going to take to the framer."

I whipped out my envelope that contained the three prints. One was Little Redbird on the Chinese-red background. Pretending I had included it by mistake, I snatched it back from him, saying, "Oh, this one is no good. It's one of his rejects."

"What do you mean—reject?" he asked, taking the picture from me and examining it.

"He made a mistake in printing. He says it's photographically a disaster. He'd have a fit if he knew I was showing it to anyone."

He looked at me incredulously, with a slight lift of the eyebrows that meant he felt he was obviously dealing with a couple of art ignoramuses. "Tell your husband he's crazy," he said. "This happens to be quite lovely as a work of art. Doesn't he know that artistically some of a photographer's best work is his mistakes?"

"That's what John Morris told him," I said.

"Of course. Now, how many more bird pictures does your husband have on hand?"

"Quite a few, but he doesn't have them all printed."

"Would he be interested in having an exhibit of them? I've never done a photographic exhibit, but I've been thinking about it. I've been to several in New York and Los Angeles and I want to do one next season. I'd like to do a hummingbird show if he has enough pictures. I think they would be very salable."

"We don't know anything about exhibits. What is the procedure?" I asked.

He explained about the costs of brochures and invitations to his client list, and the opening-night cocktail reception, which was not obligatory, he said, but he would highly recommend it. The gallery, of course, would take a commission on the pictures sold.

"What kind of price would your husband set on the pictures?" he asked.

"I haven't the vaguest idea." I didn't tell him my husband was accustomed to giving them away. "What would you suggest?"

"I'd say they should be in a price range of $300 to $700, possibly more, depending on whether they would be shown and sold as originals or in limited editions of fifteen or twenty-five or so, whatever number he would choose to print."

My heart jumped at the nice price range, but sank at the

thought of Russell trying to turn out prints in large numbers. He had problems enough with limited editions of one.

"How many would you need for an exhibit?" I asked.

"At least thirty-five or forty. And," he added, "they'll need to have better frames than these. You can't show fine work in tacky frames."

That was a bit of a blow, considering the framing bill I had just paid. But I was consoled with the thought that at least he was genuinely impressed with Russell's pictures. He recommended another framer, told me to talk it over with my husband and let him know if he was interested in having an exhibit of his work, and said he would schedule a date for two weeks during the next fall or winter season.

I hurried home to tell Russell the good news. He was sitting at his think-shop table in the Hummingbird Room with his electronic gear strewn all around, working on a gadget.

"Guess what! You're going to have an exhibit and they're going to sell your pictures."

"Yes? How much?" He didn't look up from his gadget.

"Three to seven hundred dollars. Isn't it terrific?"

"Sure. I guess so." Then he looked up and said, "See what I'm building. It's a new switch for my solenoid. I found an old motorcycle battery in my junk box. I don't know where it came from, but I tore it apart and it's coming in handy with this gadget. I hope it works. . . ."

"Why aren't you listening to me? Wouldn't you like to sell your pictures? Wouldn't you like to have them exhibited in an art gallery?"

"Sure I'd like to sell them. I don't know about having an exhibit." His nose was down on the solenoid switch again and he asked, again without looking up, "Did you tell the man about my eyes?"

"No. Of course not."

"Are you positive? I'll bet you did."

"I did not."

"I don't want anybody giving me an exhibit or buying my pictures just because I can't see," he said.

I felt a twinge of both sadness and compassion. I could understand why he wanted nobody's sympathy. He would rather give his pictures away. He needed reassurance that his pictures would be accepted on their merits. It was a situation that had to be handled delicately and I only made matters worse by blurting out, "The man even liked your Little Redbird picture. He says you're crazy to throw that one away."

"Oh, no! You didn't show him that one!"

"But he said it's beautiful, one of your best. . . ."

"That shows he doesn't know too much about photography," Russell said.

That was the end of that exhibit.

Meanwhile, with the encouragement and prodding of friends and strangers alike, I simply took it upon myself, as unobtrusively as possible, to get Russell ready for an exhibit of his pictures, which I was sure was going to happen sometime. He had other tentative offers that he wouldn't follow up. A friend of a friend knew a gallery owner in New York . . . another in Los Angeles . . . another in Laguna Beach. . . . If Russell wanted an exhibit, it could be arranged, we were assured. Another gallery in Palm Springs was also interested. Russell wasn't.

I recruited a few friends as co-conspirators in reshaping his mental attitude toward a gallery exhibit and needling him to make more prints for framing.

The printing, of course, presented a very real physical problem that he could not do very much more about than what he was already doing. At best, on the good days when everything went right in the darkroom—color exposures, temperatures, densitometer, and his blurred pinpoint eyesight—he might with luck turn out one or two good five-by-seven or eight-by-ten color prints in a single day, compared with the hundred he could do easily in a day when he could see. Now there were days and weeks at a time when he could not see well enough for printing. Or, as he called it, "wasting paper." He might spend a week or two getting one good small print. The larger ones took much longer. It would take forever to get forty pictures printed and framed for an exhibit!

There was no exhibit scheduled yet, except in my head. But I began deviously sneaking off pictures to be framed. As I brought them home, one or two at a time, Russell would look at them and say, "That's a beautiful framing job. But what are you going to do with them?"

"You're going to have an exhibit," I kept telling him. And all I got out of him was, "Okay."

Then one evening Kay Obergfel, who owned a small prestigious gallery in Palm Desert, whirled into our house and briskly announced, "I came to see these bird pictures that everyone's talking about."

Russell was in his backyard workshop. I left Kay looking at the pictures and hurried back to tell him, "Kay Obergfel is here. She's interested in your pictures. You should come out and say hello to her."

"I'd rather not, if you don't mind," he said. "It's better if I'm not there. You can talk to her."

We both knew Kay Obergfel's reputation as an art patron and entrepreneur. Her gallery was a showplace for a select few American and European artists and sculptors, most of whom she had discovered and launched on the way to success. She was known to have a shrewd head for business and a sharp eye for talent, both extending far beyond the boundaries of southern California. In art circles from coast to coast and in Europe the Kay Obergfel Gallery was recognized as one of the accepted places for artists to be "discovered."

"John Morris told me I should have a look at these birds," she said, as her sharp sea-green eyes darted critically from pic-

ture to picture. Then, "But these don't look like photographs.
They look like paintings. And these," she said, pointing to my
two Calliope misnomers, "look like watercolors. . . . And
this"—the Little Redbird now beautifully framed—"is lovely.
How did he do this?"

"I don't know." I was not about to tell Kay Obergfel it was
a mistake.

"You know," she said, "I've never given a photographic
show at my gallery and I've always said I never would. I only
do fine art, Impressionist paintings, sculpture. My clients don't
buy things like drawings or watercolors or lithographs. I don't
know anything about photography, but I've just made up my
mind. I'm going to have an exhibit of these birds. How many
pictures does he have?"

At the moment she was looking at about fifteen framed.

"How many do you need?"

"About thirty-five or forty."

Russell came in just as she was leaving.

"Congratulations," Kay said to him. "You're having an exhibit at my gallery. Your bird pictures are stunning."

He thanked her politely, and as soon as she was out of the
door, he asked, "Did she really like the pictures?"

"That's a silly question. Kay Obergfel doesn't do exhibits
for anybody unless she likes the work, and it has to be pretty
good for her to like it."

"She's not going to have one of those parties, is she?"

117

"Probably. She always does."

Kay Obergfel's gallery openings were glittering social events, attended by the rich and elite from the desert's winter colony as well as Hollywood celebrities. I had covered many of them for my newspaper column. But big social affairs were anathema to Russell. He never went to them if he could avoid it even when he could see well, and then it was usually only when he had a photographic assignment to cover a party.

I wasn't surprised when he informed me, "Well, I'm not going to any opening-night party. I think it's nice if she wants to exhibit my pictures, but you can tell her to skip the party."

"But you have to be there for your own opening."

"She can have the opening without me. I'm not going to any party." He was adamant.

"Okay." I figured I could handle that problem later. A more immediate problem was producing forty hummingbird pictures, all signed, numbered, named, and framed for his exhibit. We had only four months in which to do this. Many of those already framed were, in Russell's opinion, not good enough for an exhibit, and if he did not like them he would not sign his name to them. I enlisted the help of a friend, Caroline Rogers, who came by regularly once or twice a week, looked through his pictures, and cudgeled him into signing them on the pretense that she wanted them for her own private collection—which she called "Russell's Rejects."

"I'm papering my walls with Russell's Rejects," she told him. "Here, sign this one."

He was amused and of course pleased at her interest. He happily gave her any pictures she wanted and Caroline would drop them off at the framer's for me on her way home.

John Morris would come by occasionally and lend a hand in the conspiracy by picking out another picture or two that *he* liked—and when John Morris liked them there was never any argument from Russell.

But his conspicuous lack of enthusiasm for having an exhibit puzzled all our friends. "Aren't you thrilled? Aren't you excited?" they kept asking.

"Sure. But I'll be glad when it's over."

He couldn't be rushed or pushed with the printing. I began to worry. "Can't you get some of your photographer friends to help you with the printing?" I asked. That was a silly question, too, which I realized the instant it was out. What he was doing might as well have been Egyptian hieroglyphics to them. They would have been delighted to help if they had known how, and they did help in many other ways—taking pictures of him at work and with his hummingbird pictures for our brochures and publicity, driving him uptown for photo supplies, assisting both of us in the selection of pictures for the brochures as well as the layout and makeup. A printer friend made the brochures and invitations for us at cost. It was heartwarming the way friends pitched in to help. At least they were enthusiastic, even if Russell wasn't.

They also helped him adjust to the idea of going to his own party.

The opening was scheduled for Easter weekend, and for weeks in advance it generated a great deal of public interest and curiosity.

Kay Obergfel's upcoming "gala Easter premiere," as she called it, of a photographic show called *Hummingbirds: Self-Portraits,* was gathering momentum as her Big Event of the season, for several reasons. For one thing, her invitations and all the publicity announced this as her "first showing of photographic art." For another—Hummingbirds? Self Portraits? Birds taking their own pictures? In art and social circles this all added up to a rather offbeat thing for Kay Obergfel to be doing. Furthermore, she was giving the red-carpet treatment to an unknown *photographer*—a big cocktail reception at the gallery, a dinner party at the Thunderbird Country Club. Such opening-night furbelows were usually reserved for her most important painters and sculptors.

These were by invitation only, of course, and not publicized in advance, but in a small town word gets around. Who was this hummingbird man who could get birds to take their own pictures and rate a show at Kay Obergfel's gallery? Our telephone began jingling with calls from the press, from bird-watchers, from people we didn't know who wanted to come to the opening.

The Exhibit

A wealthy socialite called and said, "I know about your husband's opening. We're not invited. We're never invited to Kay Obergfel's openings. But my husband is interested in photography and he wants to see these pictures, so we're coming anyway."

And they did! So did about four hundred other invited guests, and a few more uninvited ones. The combination of Kay Obergfel and hummingbirds proved to be a surefire attention getter. It was the largest crowd she had ever had in her gallery for an opening in its twenty years of operation, she told me later (she keeps tab by names in her guest book and amount of liquor consumed), though the number of invitations she sends out is always approximately the same.

Many I'm sure came out of curiosity: to see why photographs of hummingbirds would be exhibited in a gallery noted for the works of John Morris, Jack Baker, painter-sculptor Gant Gaither, Vasilli Lambrinos (a Greek primitive painter), and the noted sculptor Tomás Concepción, whose exhibition had just ended.

And many came solely to see the hummingbird pictures. None of us had any idea that photographs of hummingbirds would attract so much attention or that there were so many bird lovers around.

No one in the milling crowd that night, except close friends and family, knew that the honored guest could not see. It would have been easy to exploit a blind man's photographic exhibit. This was one point we had stipulated from the beginning, that

Russell's visual impairment was not to be mentioned in the gallery's advertising or publicity releases.

Kay herself was unaware of the extent of his sight loss until it became necessary for me to tell her. He had almost backed out of coming at the last minute because he did not want people to know he couldn't see. He admitted it to me in a rare moment of disconsolate opening-night "stage fright."

"Everyone keeps asking why I'm not excited or enthusiastic," he said. "I'll tell you why. I don't know all those people who'll be there. I won't be able to recognize their voices if I don't know them. I won't be able to move around and shake hands the way you're supposed to. I'll be stumbling and bumping into people. Or I'll have to stand in the same spot and have someone beside me all the time to tell me who the people are, and that would look terrible. Then they'd know. . . . I don't want people staring at me or feeling sorry for me or thinking the pictures are good just because they were done by a blind photographer. And if I go, if I'm there, everybody's going to know."

"Nobody's going to know," I assured him. And again friends volunteered their services as Russell's Watch Squad for the evening. We mapped tactical and strategic positions for the evening as carefully as an army combat team. Two husky male friends were assigned to stand guard at his elbows, left and right, to direct traffic in front of him rather than to the side or back, and ready to catch him if he stumbled or fell in the jostling. Three others, pretty females, were assigned to *mingle,* listen to names and tidbits of information, and guide people to Russell, saying in a surprised tone, "Oh, here you are!"

Kay had strategically placed a chair at one end of the gallery for him to sit in if he wanted to—"We'll just say you're tired," she whispered—or for him to stand behind and hang on to. Fortunately, a pretty three-year-old child whose mother brought her to the cocktail reception because she couldn't find a baby-sitter plopped herself in the chair and stayed there most of the evening. The guests naturally assumed the chair was there for the child—and the honored guest hovering close to it was probably her father.

All of our helper-friends, the Watch Squad, were well acquainted with Russell's eye problem, knew how and when to direct a handshake, an introduction, a chitchat conversation, eye and head movements, and most important on this occasion, his body movements. Our pilot friend, Gordon Hansen, for example, whom we had appointed as Russell's chief bodyguard for the evening, neatly nudged him toward an outstretched hand or away from a well-wisher who crowded in too close. Rusell was terrified, he admitted later, of bumping into one of the tall white pedestals on which reposed the small, exquisite Tomás Concepción bronze statues that Kay had left standing because, she said, "They complement the hummingbirds. They seem to go together." The little bronzes had big price tags on them, from $5,000 to $10,000.

123

But Russell got through the evening without knocking any of them over. Throughout it all he was the star of the show, a reversal of roles that was brand-new to both of us. As reporter and photographer we had covered many such social soirees, had written about and photographed some of the celebrities who were now crowding around him.

In the popping of flashbulbs, by photographers he had once trained in the business, Russell recognized the voices of people he knew from the past, friends who had come from great distances to be there for his opening. It was overwhelming, heartwarming, and also a bit unbelievable. We even sold a few pictures. By the end of the first week we had sold enough to almost pay the framers.

There were a number of raised eyebrows at the price tag on the Little Redbird picture. I had purposely marked it $1,500 on one side and N.F.S. on the other, meaning "Not for Sale." One woman remarked haughtily, "We are accustomed to paying outrageous prices for everything these days, but I must say I have never seen prices like this on a *photograph*!"

I politely turned the tag over and showed her the N.F.S. initials, explaining that the picture was definitely not for sale at any price; the photographer didn't want to sell it.

"Why not?" she asked.

"His wife has a sentimental attachment to it."

It was a great tribute to Russell that so many longtime friends from Chicago and northern Michigan flew in especially for his opening. There was a contingent from the Interlochen Fine Arts Center, where he had worked and taught for many years. He could not see the eyes filled with pride and tears of happiness for him that night, but he recognized all their voices.

Among the most special guests at the gallery opening were Russell's two doctors in Palm Springs, with their wives, and I'll never forget the look of amazement on their faces when they saw the display of photographs by their patient, who was medically considered to be blind. I watched them glance over at Russell with puzzled expressions as though there must be some mistake. There wasn't time for much discussion in the crowded gallery, but within the next few days both doctors called and came to our house to congratulate Russell—and I suspect to see for themselves how he could be photographing hummingbirds.

Dr. Burton J. Winston, the internist who has treated him for years—and also took bedside lessons in photography from him— was fascinated with the seeing-eye bird shooter.

While Russell wasn't listening, he gave me a word picture of his patient that I cherish. "You know," he said, "he has always been a very unusual patient. He has never been a denier. Some people refuse to admit they are ill. Russell is a severe diabetic who has had severe complications that normal diabetics do not have. But one thing I noticed from the beginning was that, no matter what happened to him, he always had a smile

125

on his face when he came out of it. He would regain consciousness or relief from pain and then there was the smile. And
though he couldn't see, his eyes always sparkled."

He paused a moment, then added, "All those times we dis-
cussed photography, he always spoke about it in the past tense.
I knew he was out of business because he couldn't see. When
you've known someone for years as a has-been and then you're
invited to a show of his work—well, I must admit it was a bit
of a shock. At first I thought this couldn't be the same person."

But no one was more astounded than our ophthalmologist,
Dr. Kenneth A. Grow, who knew Russell's amount of "visual
acuity" better than anyone.

"I was frankly aghast when I saw those pictures," he said.
"Knowing his eyes as I do, it is unbelievable that a man with so
little vision can do this. I know the optic areas that have been
destroyed. I know his visual field loss. There is no way to explain it medically, but he obviously sees better than it is possible
for him to see.

"According to his medical history, with his amount of sight
loss he isn't supposed to be able to see.

"Yet here is a man without sight who can see better than
most of us. And he's making other people see things they've
never seen before. We don't have all the answers," he said,
"but I think in Russell's case the answer has to come from
within, from something besides visual acuity. From inspiration,
the desire and will to do something. We can grade the amount

of visual acuity, 5 percent, 3 percent, and so on, but there is no way to grade the amount of inspiration that makes a man do what he does. This makes the difference between sight and vision. The two are not the same.

"Russell did not depend on his visual acuity to take these pictures. And they tell us something about the magnificence of man, how some can cope in a crisis. Some can't cope. They fall apart. Others soar off—into the heights."

CHAPTER SEVEN

The Awakening

The success of the hummingbird show changed our world in many ways. For Russell it was a greater triumph than anything he had achieved when he had twenty-twenty vision. It was a triumph tinged with the bright and the bitter. Almost overnight he had gained more recognition for his work than had come to him in all his other years put together.

But it wasn't done with the single flick of a camera shutter. For him "overnight" represented three years and millions of flicks for the forty hummingbird pictures he consented to have shown to the public. It was a minuscule creative output by ordinary standards, but enough to awaken in him a sleeping colossus of inner "seeing power" that neither of us knew was possible.

In telling his story I have at times felt a rather awkward

sense of responsibility, realizing the danger of imparting false hopes to the millions of the "visually handicapped," as they are known. We have been told that the pattern of defeat is common among the sightless. They are enslaved by a certain stigma attached to the affliction. Blind people are frequently treated as though they are invisible. The very words *blind* and *blindness* seem to conjure up the worst in our imagination. For some they seem to be almost on a par with *terminal illness*. Much that is written about blindness, like cancer, tends to be overly negative, melodramatic, with emphasis on the "tragedy" and "hopelessness" of life.

But blindness is not the worst thing that can happen to a person. For many it can be a beginning in understanding and valuing life. And thousands of sightless people, it should be remembered, do lead useful and productive lives. Russell is not the only one.

It is generally recognized, however, that the older a person is at the onset of blindness, the more difficult it is for him to adjust. I think it was more difficult for Russell because of his profession. He had spent most of his adult life in photography, a skill in which a basic requirement is good eyesight. I believe that his philosophical reconciliation—*not* resignation—to a world he could not change was itself the passkey to an inner world that he could and did change.

Once he had faced up to the truth of the word we both abhorred and had tried to erase from our consciousness, he was

129

freed from the bonds that enslave the blind. When he accepted his sight loss as a fact of life, he could get on with the business of making the most of it, turning an adversity into an advantage.

The three years of patience, perseverance, sheer guts and determination that went into the making of his forty hummingbird pictures were worth it for his shining hour of rebirth as a photographer, doing the kind of work he loved most. The exhibit itself was an accomplishment of combined skills, physical endurance, and fortitude. But more important was the change it brought in him.

The transformation was obvious and incredible to everyone who knew him. Suddenly, surprisingly, a new self emerged. It was as complete a human metamorphosis as any I have ever seen.

To say that it started with the hummingbirds may sound melodramatic, but it happens to be true.

Trying to photograph the hummingbirds without seeing them was the best thing that could have happened to him, both physically and psychologically. They were a challenge to him. They made him strain to use his eyes *and* his mind in ways that he had never done before. As a result, he learned how to do more things better than he did them when he could see—and better than many with twenty-twenty vision. They restored his confidence in himself, opened a new world and a new career with his cameras, and revived his exuberance for life by making him prove to himself that he *could* still take pictures. The hummingbirds brought him the rare gift of vision without sight, and, as Dr. Grow said, the two are not synonymous.

But almost as amazing to me were the other things he learned to do by himself and for himself, the latent skills, talents, and interests he discovered within himself—not all as beautiful and wondrous as his world of hummingbirds but more basic to the necessities of everyday life.

He took over certain household chores that he did not know how to do, did not particularly want to do, and could not really see to do. But he forced himself to do them anyway, just to prove he could, with the result that he became an expert at some of them. He assumed the multitude roles of chief cook and bottle-washer, gardener, pool man, repairman, electrician, plumber, and tile-setter at our house, doing and creating in a way he never did when he had sight.

There have been problems, especially in *my* kitchen, which he has made *his*. Once I walked into find him whipping up an egg and mushroom omelette in a mixing bowl—with one foot in a raw egg on the floor.

"You've dropped an egg!" I yelped.

"No, I didn't. It must have rolled off. I was wondering what happened to that egg," he said blithely.

He breaks a lot of dishes, drops spoons down the Insinkerator (garbage disposal), spills and splatters, but mops up his own mess, which is more than most men do in the kitchen. In the process he has managed, with incredible patience, to turn out gourmet dishes that I wouldn't dream of attempting. In fact, for our holiday dinner parties, especially Thanksgiving and Christmas turkey feasts, I am banned from the kitchen except to fill the salt and pepper shakers, creamer, and butter plate.

Previously the extent of my husband's culinary skills was making instant coffee and frozen orange juice. He started to cook only after he lost his sight.

How did he learn to do all these things? The same way he learned to photograph hummingbirds, by facing the fact that he had a problem. He couldn't see with his eyes. So he trained himself to see in other ways.

"A lot of seeing is in the mind," he explained. "You can *learn* to see. Anyone can learn to see better than they do if they try."

He began doing most of our grocery shopping, although he had never done it before. He loathes supermarkets because he is always bumping into people. But he decided that doing the marketing would be good for him whether he liked it or not; it was better for him to learn to cope with the crowds of shoppers than to avoid them; it was good exercise in self-discipline and patience, two qualities that he considers basic requirements in adjusting to subnormal vision; it could be an important aid to self-development, self-reliance, and independence in many ways. He prefers to do the marketing alone, with no help from me. If I drive him to the market, I have to wait in the car.

He has learned to pick out certain items on shelves and counters by the color of the label, the size of the can or the box, the feel of a cut of meat. He knows exactly where everything is in the store, from soaps and soups to water chestnuts. He has trained his memory to add up the bill as he goes along so that he will have the proper amount of cash in hand without any fumbling at the check-out counter.

More important, he has learned to walk from our house to the market and back wheeling the grocery cart, crossing streets with traffic signals he can't see, without being struck by a car.

As he explains it, "When I'm walking, I use my ears and my feet to see with."

Mostly he uses the balls of his feet and his toes (his shoes in those parts are worn thin) to *feel* the street curbs, so he knows when he comes to the end of a block, a corner, or an intersection. Usually he stands and waits and *listens* for cars and for people to come near him; he can tell by the sounds— footsteps, voices, movements—when pedestrians start crossing the street, and then he goes along with them. If they are directly in front of him he can sometimes follow their shadowy images.

He has never liked anyone, not even close friends or me, to take him by the arm or elbow and guide him "It's irritating to have people try to help you. It makes you feel like *they* think you're a cripple, and that's not the right attitude for other people to have," he has often told me. And he has frequently chastened me for worrying too much about him when, for example, he's climbing around on ladders or on the roof.

"I don't need to be led around in a noose or held back from doing whatever I'm capable of doing. You have to have independence, and I'm perfectly capable of taking care of myself. I know what I can and can't do," he reminds me.

There was something mystifying and wonderful in the new capabilities he discovered daily in the hidden channels of his mind. There seemed to be no end to the marvels, great and small, unleashed from my husband's head after the hummingbirds came.

No sooner did he have his seeing-eye bird shooter working than he began building an insect shooter and butterfly net. He plans to add butterflies, dragonflies, and bumblebees to his hummingbird portfolio.

Meanwhile, as I write these lines, he is preparing for his next hummingbird exhibit. And this time he *is* excited. Kay Obergfel called to tell him she wants more hummingbirds for her opening show next season. They are to be featured along with the paintings of artist John Morris.

Most mystifying of all the changes in our lives is Russell's continuing relative remission of severe physical problems. The astonishing fact is that his eye hemorrhaging has stopped and he has not been to Colorado since he began photographing hummingbirds, now going on four years. Nor has he been in the hospital with diabetic complications.

I do not dismiss lightly the medical realities, having lived with them for a long time. But if his health has not actually improved, at least it *seems* to be no worse. His eyesight may have diminished, but I think he sees better, or at least as well, as he did three years ago. It may be only wishful thinking, of course. But the important thing is to hang on to the dream. Silly as it sounds, it really sometimes comes true. The other day Russell saw a hummingbird perched on a top branch of our orange tree.

"Look at him preen! Can you see him?" he said.

"*You're* asking *me?*"

It wasn't the flash of color, the sound of chic-chics, or the whir of wings that he recognized. It was a hummingbird, and he saw it before I did.

"I can see its image against the sky," he explained.

I called him out of his workshop one day and absent-mindedly asked, "What kind of bird is *that?*" pointing to a big bird loudly warbling on our TV cable wire.

He looked around and cheerfully reminded me, "Honey, you know I don't see very well. How would I know what kind of a bird it is?"

"But can't you tell by its singing?"

"No."

"You really can't see it?"

"No."

"But it's ten times bigger than a hummingbird. How do you know when you see a hummingbird?"

"When I see a hummingbird, I know that's what it is, a hummingbird."

Not the least of our new-found pleasures in life has been the discovery of bird-watching as an absorbing interest in and of itself. To our surprise there was a genuine thrill in learning to recognize some of the hummingbirds at our house by the "field marks" in the books. I can understand now why serious "birders" are as dedicated as chess addicts. We no longer call our hummingbirds Cassius or Freddy or Flirty Bird. Instead, Russell asks "*What* is it?" and I tell him if it is an Anna's or a Costa's or a Calliope. Recently we've had a little Calliope holding forth in the orange tree, and now I know that he *is* a Calliope because of his purple distended bib against a white throat. . . .

He dances and dangles in front of our noses, hovers at our heads, swoops at our feet. "He's becoming almost as friendly as that first little bird," Russell said.

He has never been able to see my favorite of all the hummingbirds, the little Rufous with his fiery throat and bright orange tail feathers. The Rufous makes only a brief stopover, two to three weeks, in his migration from Alaska to Mexico.

"Look! Can't you see it?" I have called hundreds of times
The other day he showed me a roll of film he developed. To my

surprise he had caught a Rufous, with its bright orange tail outspread.

"*That's* a Rufous," I told him, "and you have to print it."

He made a print. It was the first time he had seen a Rufous hummingbird tail. "It is beautiful, isn't it?" he said. He made several more prints; the colors weren't just right; he'll have the Rufous in his next hummingbird exhibit and if ornithologists say it's an Allen's, never mind, we came close!

Our Hummingbird Room now is cluttered with slide rules, color charts, art materials, photo equipment, and negatives for testing experiments in transferring the hummingbirds to canvas and putting them against backgrounds of four-color water.

Russell explained that while he's photographing the water, it will change colors as it moves—when he learns how to do it.

"It will make beautiful backgrounds for the hummingbirds," he said.

"What do you think the ornithologists will say about *that*?"

"Well, maybe they won't like it. But I'm not making pictures for ornithologists," he said.

"Where are you going to get the water?" I asked.

"We're going back to Tahiti. There's sure no water around here to photograph."

"But there are no hummingbirds in Tahiti."

"That's okay. The water is only for background. I'm using the sprinklers for tests, but what I really need are some big rolling waves in reds and yellows and blues and greens, or purples and golds. I can get any color I want when I have it all figured out."

Our patio has now turned into a color-testing laboratory with water sprinklers spraying in different angles of sunlight. And there is not the slightest doubt in my mind that, when we come back from Tahiti, we'll have big rolling waves in reds and yellows and all the glittering colors of the rainbow for our hummingbirds.

Often as I stand watching in tiptoed wonder at the sunburst explosion of his inner powers beyond seeing, I ask myself the same question others have asked: How can he do this? How is it possible?

Then I remember, *Humingbirds can't fly but they do.* And so it is with him.

Who can explain how miracles happen? Who can explain birth or rebirth or an awakening of spirit and mind? Who knows why or how a new self is born in a man because he suddenly saw a hummingbird?

Hummingbirds:
Self-Portraits

by Russell Ogg

Hummingbirds: Self-Portraits

by Russell Ogg

The pictures presented here are not photographic illustrations of hummingbirds as required in the science or study of ornithology. I am not a nature or bird photographer or a photo illustrator.

I prefer pictures of birds and insects in flight, or with some motion. I do not care for the full-front, static look of pinned-back bird and butterfly wings, which I realize are necessary if the aim is to identify details of various species. I am not concerned with this in photographing hummingbirds. What I have tried to do is catch their beauty in motion.

I use a Mamiya RB67 camera to take the pictures of the hummingbirds because of the larger negative size, $2\frac{1}{4}$ x $2\frac{3}{4}$. I have also adapted a Speed Graphic lens (127 mm Ektar) with a solenoid using nine volts to trip the shutter.

141

He Saw a Hummingbird

The shutter is tripped by the hummingbird when it flies through a light beam. I have developed and built my own light sensor that triggers a relay that sets off the camera shutter.

The first sensor I made used a cadmium sulfide photocell, but this took in too large an area and I was unable to catch the bird in the negative frame, so I changed to a phototransistor placed in a small black plastic tube and now have a light beam about two to three millimeters in diameter. This permits me to center the bird in the picture frame very accurately. The light source is a small flashlight placed on a tripod about two feet in front of the sensor. (See page 143 for the schematic of the light sensor, which is easy to build.)

I use three strobe lights, one above the camera lens pointing down, another on the side, and one at the side and below the lens pointing up. This gives a light from all directions, which will generally pick up the iridescence of the colors.

It takes an exposure of at least two- to three-thousandths of of a second to stop the wing movements of the birds. Most strobes have a speed of about one-thousandth of a second, so I built my own. But recently I found that the Vivitar 283 strobes are very fast and powerful enough so that a stop of f/22 is necessary when they are used about two feet from the picture area. The sensing element of the strobe must be directed toward a background about two to four feet behind the picture area. For the background I use a painted window shade that can be rolled up and down.

LIGHT-ACTIVATED PHOTOTRANSISTOR RELAY

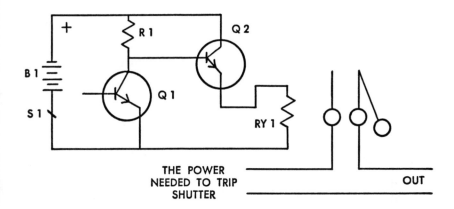

Parts List *

B 1—Battery, 9 volts
Q 1—FPT Phototransistor (276-130)
Q 2—2N222 NPN Transistor (276-2009)
R 1—100,000 OHM Resistor
RY 1—Miniature SPDT Relay (275-004)
S 1—SPST Miniature Switch

*Radio Shack catalog numbers are in parentheses

Hummingbirds:
Self-Portraits

LITTLE REDBIRD

The one who started it all.
    Photographic note: Total disaster. Darkroom mistake in printing.
            Speed: 1/1000 of a second.
            Time: Evening.
            Ornithological note: Anna's? Costa's? Tell us.
            Price: $1,500. Not for sale.
            Owner: Norma Lee Browning Ogg

FLOWER KISSER

Brazilians call the hummingbird *beija-flor,* which means literally "kiss-flower." Thus the hummingbird is known as a "flower kisser." Here the flower kisser pulls beak from blossom and goes into reverse, starting a backward half-roll. (*Courtesy of Jessie V. and W. Clement Stone, Winnetka, Illinois*)

HUMMER AND HIBISCUS

The most popular picture in the exhibit was this Tom Thumb humming-bird, perched and eyeing the red blossom. The hummingbird's tiny feet are not designed for walking or hopping around, but for clamping onto twigs and perches. (*Courtesy of Jessie V. and W. Clement Stone, Win-netka, Illinois*)

SILHOUETTE

Is it photography? The sculptor Tomás Concepción called it a "beautiful work of abstract art."

Photographic note: The two front strobe lights (out of four) did not go off, due to a mechanical fault.

Some of our best are mistakes.

(*Courtesy of John Morris, Palm Springs, California*)

AERIALIST

Hummers can fly backwards, upside down, sideways. They can do complete barrel rolls and half-rolls, hover motionless on invisible wings, twist,
bend, curl, swivel, or zigzag. Note the expression on this hummer's face as
he starts into backward somersault. (*Courtsey of Mr. and Mrs. Wade
Barnes, New York City*)

SYMPHONY IN BLUE

Hummingbirds can't sing, but the humming noise of their wings is the reason they're called hummingbirds. This hummer reminds us of a symphony conductor with arms raised. (*Courtesy of Dr. and Mrs. Kenneth A. Grow, Palm Springs, California*)

HUMMINGBIRD AND BEE

Hummingbirds are completely fearless of man, beast, or bees, and they don't like them freeloading from their sugarwater bottles. This picture attracted a great deal of attention, since it is rare to get a picture of a hummingbird and bee together. (*Courtesy of Mrs. William [Dorothy] Siegel, Chicago*)

TROCHILIDAE

This multiple exposure took a lot of time and several rolls of film. It's one of the favorites of gallery owner Kay Obergfel.

Trochilidae is the family name for hummingbirds. It comes from the Greek, though the Greeks were not familiar with hummingbirds. (*Courtesy of Kay Obergfel Gallery, Palm Desert, California*)